Do Grow

Start with 10 simple vegetables

Alice Holden

Published by
The Do Book Company 2013
Works in Progress Publishing Ltd
thedobook.co

Text copyright © Alice Holden 2012
Photographs copyright © Nick Hand,
Jon Heslop and Alice Holden
Illustrations © Millie Marotta 2012

A CIP catalogue record for this book
is available from the British Library

ISBN 978-1-907974-02-1

5 7 9 10 8 6 4

To find out more about our company,
books and authors, please visit
thedobook.co

5% of our proceeds from the sale
of this book is given to The Do
Lectures to help it achieve its aim
of making positive change
thedolectures.com

Cover designed by James Victore
Book designed and typeset by Ratiotype

Printed and bound at Livonia Print
on Munken, an FSC-certified paper

'I think the cauliflower
more beautiful than the rose.'

—

Uncle Monty, *Withnail and I*

Book Co

Books in the series:

Available in print and digital formats
from bookshops, online retailers
or via our website:
thedobook.co

To hear about events and forthcoming
titles, you can find us on Facebook,
on Twitter and Instagram @dobookco,
or subscribe to our newsletter

Contents

For Pip, who visited me in my gardens.

Fforest poly-tunnel, W. Wales

Introduction

This book does not tell you how to grow every vegetable under the sun. This is not through a desire to be overly prescriptive. It's just that when confronted with limitations of space and overwhelmed by choice, where do we begin?

My belief is that if we focus on fewer things and get a good return for our scale, we will be encouraged to grow more of our own food.

Over the years I have worked for many commercial vegetable growers. They have grown their crops organically and produced a great range of them in order to build biodiversity and resilience. I've noticed that if faced with limited space, growers focus on certain crops. These tend to be vegetables that are of higher value, things that grow quickly and keep giving. Take the cabbage: to grow one cabbage from seed can take around a third of a year and it will take up a fair amount of ground. Alternatively, lettuces take around six weeks and, if harvested correctly, will keep producing tender, delicious leaves. In my opinion this gives a far better return and greater pleasure to grow on a smaller, garden scale.

The same can be said of other staple crops – potatoes, onions and large carrots. These are things that it makes sense to grow on a larger scale, as most people simply do not have the land required. However, if our aim is to produce some of our diet, then anyone with a little space can make an important contribution to what they eat. Already many people are doing this and there has been a significant shift.

This book is designed to encourage you to get started and produce a harvest that you can eat! So to keep it manageable I've focused on just 10 things:

1. Hardy herbs
2. Tender herbs
3. Summer salads
4. Winter salads
5. Chard and spinach
6. Beetroot
7. Courgettes and cucumbers
8. Tomatoes
9. Beans
10. Winter greens

This selection is, like that of so many growers, based on value for space (the smaller the space you have, start with the things higher on the list), ease of growth and intensity of flavour when fresh. These are all vegetables that I grow year after year, regardless of where I might be living.

There are plenty of advantages to growing food at home. First and foremost, vegetables do not respond well to being packed, wrapped, refrigerated and trucked. The delicate and the tender, such as the summer salads and tender herbs that I've included, are best delivered straight from plant to mouth.

Sustenance becomes about the whole experience: sowing, picking, cooking, eating and the pleasure each stage of the process gives.

Change your view. Plant a garden.

Fforest garden, W. Wales

1
**Space and
Getting Started**

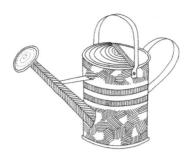

People who grow their own food are often highly knowledgeable. There are plenty of accomplished allotment holders and gardeners out there, but any of us can give it a go. Growing food is something we have done for thousands of years and we are all capable.

When I moved from the Welsh countryside back to the city, I became aware of the difficulties that confront urban dwellers, the main one being space. With my keen gardener's eye I was noticing weeds sprouting in cracks in the pavement, herbs on the balconies of tower blocks and tomato plants on doorsteps. It reminded me of what can be grown in even the smallest of spaces.

Initially, to get a sense of your growing options and what space you have available, ask yourself the following:

What size container can I fit in my space?
— A simple plant pot, a window box, a raised bed?

What conditions does my space offer?
— Is it sheltered from wind?
— Does it get much sun?
— Is there water nearby?

Do I have any decent soil?

Generally, unless you have been fortunate to inherit well-loved raised beds or garden plots full of dark earthworm-rich compost, there will be work to do! Chances are you'll find soil that has one or many of the following problems:

— rocks
— clods
— waterlogging
— compaction
— cracking
— weed cover

Soil suffers if it is not looked after, especially if it is left bare. The main problems are compaction, erosion and lack of fertility – through not replacing organic matter taken out at harvest.

Remember the law of return. In other words, as you harvest your produce, remember to replenish the soil with plenty of decent compost (more on this later). Make the most of the space that you do have by thinking about soil depth, as well as area. In fact, having a small space can be a blessing as you are forced to focus your energy efficiently. Nurturing a small area rather than fretting about taking on the earth will allow you to improve the soil and, in turn, your bounty.

In this way small can be intensive, productive, sustainable and beautiful.

YOUR ESSENTIAL TOOLKIT

I have never been one to wear appropriate clothing or kit myself out with every tool available. I prefer to make do. Some tools are essential in order to get started but really you need very little.

My basic tool kit consists of the following:
— **My hands**
— **Marigold gloves** – gloves are a very personal thing
— **Garden knife**
— **Watering can**
— **Hose pipe** I use this a lot and it is worth investing in one that is robust and does not kink
— **Wheelbarrow** to move (a LOT) of compost, weeds, seed trays
— **Bamboo canes** to support plants
— **String** to plant in straight(ish) lines, measure distances and tie plants to canes
— **Garden fork** for turning in manure and turning compost
— **Buckets** for collecting weeds
— **Spade** for moving the good earth
— **Trowel** for weeding and planting
— **Module trays** for sowing seeds
— **A pencil and lollipop sticks** to label seedlings
— **Seed compost** (preferably organic) from a garden centre
— **Rake** to break up clods of earth to make a tilth (soil suitable for planting)

And, occasionally:
— **Secateurs** for pruning
— **Bubble wrap / horticultural fleece** to protect plants from frosts
— **A notebook** to remember what I planted, where and when
— **Recycled containers** to make beer traps for slugs
— **Netting** to protect crops from the birds

This sounds like a lot of equipment but I sometimes grow on a relatively large scale. Most of the time I can get by with far less. The most useful tools to make things manageable tend to be the raised beds themselves, module trays and my hands.

Access to a greenhouse is invaluable, though you can raise most plants without one.

All plants vary yet they require similar conditions in order to grow healthily. It may seem obvious but these things are worth repeating (and I will do so throughout this book!) as they have the greatest effect upon our ability to raise crops.

When planting seeds, setting up a raised bed or trying to encourage any plant to grow, take a moment to consider the factors that enable life to flourish. The very things upon which we ourselves rely:

— Food
— Water
— Room to grow
— Shelter from the elements
— Natural light

Food for plants exists in nurtured, healthy soil. It should not be thought of as something that you add as an individual 'extra' ingredient. You want to sustain soil life by adding something balanced, something that already has the right mix of ingredients. Compost does this in an ideal way. It contains food for plants and soil micro-organisms. Compost also helps to build a structure that allows nutrients and moisture to reach plants.

Soil is complex; adding compost to it is a simple way of looking after and improving whatever you have inherited.

Raised Beds

The beauty of working on a small scale is that you can create your growing area by hand, and then manage it by hand. The best way to do this is to focus effort on improving a relatively small space. If you have room, I strongly recommend a raised bed. The creation of the raised bed is where 90 per cent of the graft lies but this toil will be well worth it for the saved exertion and abundance offered later. Hopefully, with this in mind it can be a labour of love.

By working in a confined, manageable space, we can turn the soil that it contains to make a tilth that will provide us with the best conditions into which we can plant. On a large scale cultivation is difficult and requires a lot of energy, as we are taking the ground away from its natural covered state. The invention of the plough was a momentous occasion and it is by no means chance that it is celebrated in the name of pubs across the land.

Raised beds are a brilliant way of creating an area of good-quality soil dedicated to growing vegetables. They

Pantsaeson Farm, W. Wales

provide a tangible canvas and allow you to get creative by mixing your vegetables, adding flowers, and so on.

The principal idea is that you are trying to increase the depth of fertile soil and compost in which to grow. Many people like to define the edges so that the perimeters are clear and the soil does not wash away. There are many materials, new or recycled, that you can do this with. Just make sure the soil is not coming into contact with anything toxic (e.g. chemically treated wood). But you don't have to board in raised beds – a less labour-intensive option is to just add soil depth. There are pluses and minuses to either practice but generally it comes down to what you have available and your own personal preference. I would say that with limited time, boarded-in beds work best as it is less likely that weeds and grass will encroach upon them. Psychologically, I prefer beds that are contained, as somehow they seem easier to manage. However, if you don't have the materials, time or funds available, you can still make a raised bed out of soil alone.

In the smallest instance, plant pots and window boxes are really just miniature raised beds.

Fforest Garden

WORKSHOP: HOW TO BUILD A RAISED BED

Having located a sensible space – taking into account what your plant needs in order to flourish (see page 19) – begin by measuring out your bed and the paths that run alongside it. I use sticks and string to mark out the different areas.

Distances

When measuring the various spacings I try not to get too hung up on dimensions given in a book and instead think about why a distance may be set as it is.

The width of your bed should be dictated by whether you are able to reach the centre from either side with reasonable ease without stepping on the bed itself. There will come a time when you are planting vegetables somewhere near the middle so you need to have a workable reach.

The paths around the bed are important as they will protect the soil inside from being trampled and compacted. Also, think about the future when you may need to fit a wheelbarrow down the side of the bed. This is probably going to be full of compost so also consider the position of your compost heap. You will want to avoid unnecessary distances.

The length of bed is up to you. But remember that you don't want to step on your precious plants or soil so will have to walk all the way around the bed to access the other side. The more path you have, the less space you will have for planting. It is a trade-off, convenience versus output.

As a rough guide, you can use the following measurements:
    Bed: 140 cm wide x 15 cm deep x 1.5-4 m long
    Path: about 30 cm wide

Materials

In the past I have created raised beds out of scaffold boards, recycled planks and untreated or lined railway sleepers. If using this type of material you need to make sure that the upright boards are well supported. The volume of soil within a bed exerts a lot of pressure so it's a good idea to make your structure as solid as you can. One way of doing this is by hammering posts into the ground. The boards making up the sides of your bed can then be nailed or bolted to the posts to give them strong support. Try and do this for each corner.

At other times I have created a raised bed without defined edges by simply piling up earth. I can also admit to having bought ready-made plastic kits from a garden centre. Both work fine. I like to minimise using plastics but, as with all resources, try to weigh up what is practical and will give a good life span.

The Filling

If you are building a bed on grass you don't need to dig the ground over first as long as you have enough soil to 'black out' the growth. First dig out any perennial weeds (like docks). Then put a layer of damp cardboard over the grass to block out the light and ensure any grass is killed off. Then you can start to add your soil.

When filling the beds, the greater the depth of healthy top-soil and compost, the healthier your plants. Top-soil is what makes up the upper part of your soil structure. I have worked on farms blessed with many feet of crumbly, cakey-rich soils, but it is far more likely that you will dig your spade into the ground and as you go down it will quickly become rocky and compacted. If this is the case, lift any looser top-soil from the designated path areas and spread it evenly over the bed to maximise what you do have. You will probably find you don't have large volumes of loose, earthworm-rich soil and you will need to bring some compost in from elsewhere.

Adding at least 5 cm of compost to a bed annually should keep it healthy and productive.

Pantsaeson Farm, W. Wales

2
Compost: Brown Gold

'Humus is the new green revolution base,
the brown gold to replace the black gold of oil.'

—

Vandana Shiva

Imagine a substance that had the ability to recycle old life into new. A substance that any of us could create, almost anywhere, with materials we already possessed. It is hard to believe that compost – something that looks so humble – has such miraculous attributes. Perhaps this is why we neglect to give it the elevation it deserves. I don't want to sound morbid but when I die I can't think of a better end than being put in a cardboard box where my body can gradually decompose to the earth.

Everything that was once living has the ability to break down and create new life when it dies. This way of recycling fertility and important minerals is essential when it comes to growing our food. Compost improves soil structure, helps retain water, traps carbon from the atmosphere and continually decays to help feed earthworms and other soil life.

We all have access to some organic waste. On average 40 per cent of what we send to landfill as waste could be made into useful compost. That, in time, can go onto your vegetable patch.

If you need to get your vegetable garden off to a flying start and can't wait for your compost heap to mature, there are alternatives. You can buy sacks of ready-made organic compost from garden centres. For cheaper sources your specific situation will dictate what may be available. Land being developed can be a good, cheap source of soil, though quality is not guaranteed. In the city, municipal green waste recycling plants are also a good source of affordable compost. Stables can be a rich source of fertility, but be aware that some straw is treated with chemicals that do not break down even when composted and can harm your plants. Ask if others use it for growing or source it from stables who use organic straw. All manure needs to be composted before you use it on your beds, though partially composted stable manure is fine to use as long as it is put at the bottom of the bed as a base layer.

Some of us may be lucky enough to inherit an old compost heap. If so, and the compost is nicely broken down and not full of large lumps, use it to top up your bed. If not, start making compost for the future or help what you have to break down using the composting advice overleaf.

WORKSHOP: HOW TO MAKE COMPOST

Making your own compost is a bit like making a layered cake. All the ingredients you need come from different types of organic waste from living things. This will decompose when exposed to the conditions that allow living organisms, such as worms, to break them down.

You will need a balance of carbon-rich 'brown' materials (woody things like paper) and the juicier nitrogen-rich 'green' materials (things like grass and vegetable peelings). Essentially you just need to mix it all up. The smaller your additions and the more mixing you do, the faster they will break down and become compost.

You are aiming to invite living organisms to do the hard work for you. Layering, mixing and chopping is the best way to achieve the conditions that will allow air, moisture and microbial life into your compost heap.

To make the structure, I use old pallets turned on their sides to create a little pen. You can also use chicken wire held in place by wooden stakes. Alternatively try and source a ready-made one from your local council or buy one from your local garden centre. Such structures enable compost to be piled on top of itself and packed into a small area. This helps it to gain heat and rot down. Compost run-off is high in nutrients and can be polluting to water courses so build your compost heap in areas away from any waterways. And to save your legs, ideally position it near the beds you'll be adding it to.

Ingredients

Brown waste: Woody material from spent plants; straw (that has not been treated); small twiggy bits of wood; ripped up newspaper and cardboard; wood chip and sawdust (make sure it has not been treated and is not all from conifer trees, which can be very acidic).

Green waste: Grass and other green plant waste including weeds (but avoid seed heads and roots of perennial weeds like dock, couch grass and nettle. These can be put in a bucket of water until they become unrecognisable, then put on the compost); kitchen waste like vegetable peelings, tea bags and coffee grounds; animal manure and bedding from herbivorous animals.

Other: Seaweed, wood ash (not in huge quantities), natural fibres (such as wool), broken eggshell, hair, feathers, flowers.

Things to avoid: Non-organic material like glass, plastic, metal, glossy or coloured paper, nappies and pet litter from animals that eat meat

Meat and dairy leftovers can encourage rats into compost heaps. However, I don't believe any organic matter should be sent to landfill. Councils will often compost this for you as they have more appropriate facilities. If they don't, perhaps ask them why they aren't providing this service.

A Few Points to Remember

— Covering a compost heap will speed up composting, but make sure the heap does not dry out. Water it or occasionally let in the rain.

— If you don't have time to break up materials before adding them to your heap, don't worry – in general, as long as you mix the different ingredients together, a heap will still break down. In all cases there needs to be moisture and small pockets of air made available.

— Remember, compost is full of life. If it has not got enough access to moisture and oxygen many organisms will not be able to carry out the composting process.

— If you have a small garden and produce a lot of 'green' kitchen waste but not much garden waste, non-glossy cardboard and paper can be added as a source of carbon-rich material.

— If you have a larger garden and a lot of garden waste it can be a good idea to have three heaps: one for woody stuff, one for green, and then your final heap where you layer the two.

Human Waste – the Big Taboo

While I do not recommend putting this particular kind of organic matter on our home compost heaps it is worth noting that our own human waste is potentially a hugely valuable source of both fertility and phosphorus for our world soils. Solid human waste needs to be composted under strict conditions to make sure any harmful pathogens are killed, but if we are to feed ourselves and our soils on a global basis, we need to start thinking about recycling our own waste. With the appropriate systems in place we could transform what is seen as a pollutant into something safe and useful.

If we are going to meet our future demands for food we will need to recycle every bit of organic matter we have.

Leaf Mould

Leaves can be added to compost heaps; however, they are more useful kept separate. If stacked or bagged together, leaves will be broken down by a fungus rather than by the bacteria found in compost. Old compost sacks are perfect for collecting together leaf drifts. Here they will break down into crumbly leaf mould, which acts as a good soil conditioner and is excellent at making soils better at retaining moisture. When making leaf mould make sure the leaves are damp or they will not break down. After many months it will begin to look like soil and at this point is ready for use.

Seaweed

If you live by the sea you might have access to seaweed washed up on the beach. This can add valuable minerals and structure to soil when it is composted. I tend to leave it spread outside for a while before I use it to let the rain wash away some of the salt, or simply hose it down. You can then layer it onto your compost heap. In the Scottish Hebrides, where there is a lack of normal composting material, seaweed is used layered thickly on garden beds over the winter, gradually breaking down to leave nutrient-rich compost behind.

Urine

Urine is a natural fertiliser as it contains nitrogen, potassium and phosphorus, the three basic elements required for all plant growth. Fresh urine is sterile and safe to use – dilute with water (so it's not too acidic for the worms) and add to your compost heap. This will help to stimulate activity.

Municipal Compost

In general, city councils now offer municipal compost facilities for green waste from their locality. The compost it creates is reasonably priced and sometimes free.

It's always good to use what you have where you are. In some cities there are free access points for collecting this compost. It can be of a lower quality but still aids soil condition and is an important way in which we can recycle our waste. The more we ask our councils about these services, the more they will be put on their agenda.

Worms

Worms may seem insignificant but they play a key part in maintaining the world's soils. They feed off organic matter in soil, giving out worm casts. These provide plants with easily accessible nutrients. Worms also aerate soils through the creation of their burrows. The amount of worms in soil is a good indicator of how healthy it is. Worms don't like to be disturbed but do like to be fed. Again, organic matter is your source. Place compost on top of a bed and the worms will take it down. There is no need to dig it in as the worms will do a more gentle job.

If you have a small garden and a lot of kitchen waste a

wormery is a good way of converting kitchen waste into food for your plants. You can make your own wormery in a box with air holes. Wide flat boxes are best as worms tend to work nearer the surface. Make a base of torn-up damp paper or card then add worms and organic matter. You can buy worms or add some from an existing compost heap or wormery. They like coffee grounds, tea bags, kitchen veg leftovers and soft garden waste. Avoid meat and dairy except in very small amounts. Large quantities of citrus and onion skins will make a wormery too acidic for worms, but eggshells can help add calcium to balance out the pH while also providing worms with roughage that aids their digestion. Worm activity will respond to temperature and will slow down when cold. Worms like dark, damp conditions and plenty of peace to get on with making compost.

Green Manures

We rarely produce much compost in a household. Green manures are plants such as clover, phacelia or rye that allow you to produce your own source of organic matter. Such plants do this by both adding or holding soil nutrients. The green manure plants increase organic matter content while their roots channel through the soil, improving its structure. Some can even add nitrogen to the soil in a form that plants can easily access, making your soil more fertile.

Even on a garden scale, green manures are useful to give cover to empty beds over winter. I often use clover to do this, which will both protect the soil and begin to fix nitrogen once spring arrives. Getting rid of green manure before planting is one of the few times I dig over my raised beds. I try to leave legume (e.g. peas and beans) roots in the ground so the nitrogen on its roots stays in the soil for the next crops. I have found that clover is vigorous so is easy to encourage back when you need it. However, it is also relatively easy to get rid of and sometimes I peel it back and even move it around, using it as a portable living mulch (for more on mulch, see page 104).

Soil pH

Soil pH will have an effect on whether your plants can access nutrients. Generally, for healthy vegetables and soil life, soils should have a pH that is fairly neutral, of around 6.5. An acid soil may be very fertile but the acidity will govern whether plants can access nutrients. It is a good idea to get a simple pH testing kit, available from any garden centre. I have to admit to never having done this on a garden scale because I haven't had problems with growing crops. However, if you are having difficulties it may be down to the pH. Most commonly this will be caused by having soil that is too acid, and if you suspect this you should do a soil test.

If you find your soil is too acidic, agricultural lime (naturally occurring calcium carbonate) will bring it back into balance. It can be bought from any garden centre and should be applied at the rate advised on the packet.

Alkaline soils are rare but adding compost to either soil type will help remedy any imbalance.

Remember the Law of Return

Adding compost is what you give back for all the delicious food you take away from the soil. It is also the practical and logical place to send your organic waste – vegetable peelings, egg shells, grass clippings. It's possible to

compost almost anything that was once alive. Waste only happens when we don't harness and recycle that which is valuable. It depends where we place value and what we see as useful. Council bags of leaves, ash from fires, stable manure, seaweed. Open your eyes to the resources on your doorstep.

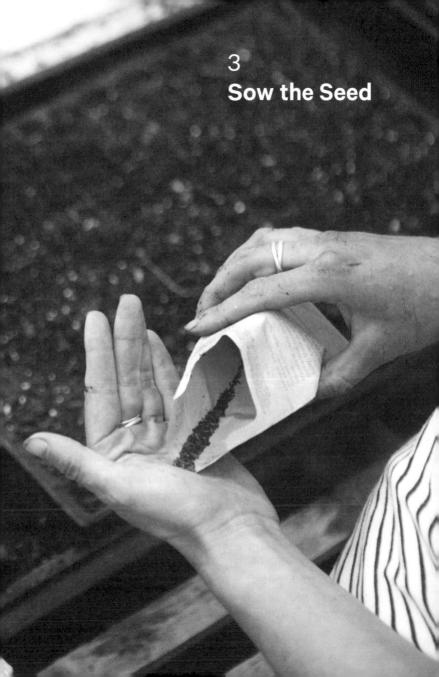

3
Sow the Seed

Not long ago my Uncle Roger, also a grower, said to me, 'Seeds want to grow.' Simple as it sounds, his comment struck me. A seed is a package of life that is well equipped to survive. It is merely waiting, lying dormant until the necessary conditions combine. With a little moisture, warmth and some light, miraculously, it will begin to wake up and start to grow.

Seed Compost

Firstly, you will need to get some seed compost from your garden centre. Sowing, potting and multi-purpose composts are different from the compost you make at home. They tend to be a mixture of materials such as coir (coconut fibre), shredded bark, sand and organic matter. These ready-made composts are balanced and weed-free, which makes them ideal for raising seeds. There are a variety of composts for different uses. Ask for a seed compost that is not too coarse so you know it will be suitable for sowing seeds.

I use organic peat-free composts so I know they have not been made using man-made fertilisers or produced from finite or polluting resources. If these are not available, I ask my garden centre if they can order some in. Alternately, you can make your own seed compost. Mix 5 parts leaf mould (that is well broken down so it resembles crumbly soil) with 2 parts clean sand.

Sourcing Your Seeds

Propagation begins with the seed so quality is important. There is no way to guarantee your seed will germinate – seed does vary and like everything is affected by the season and how it is kept. The best assurance you have is to use good seed companies – I have listed some in the Side Shoots section.

I tend to bulk-buy from seed companies, placing my order some time near the end of January. If I'm less organised I buy from independent garden centres who often have staff with a wealth of information. At the Brondesbury Garden Centre in Cardigan, Wales, I always get lots of sound advice and find I can tap into local knowledge about what is working (or not!) for fellow growers in the same area and climate.

I try to use organic seed unless I can't obtain the variety I want. Organic seed has been raised from organic plants and thus in a way that has not polluted the environment. The more we use organic varieties the more demand there will be for them, and I try to support this philosophy.

Varieties

There are a wealth of vegetable varieties available to us. Seed catalogues offer a sweet-shop array of colours, shapes and sizes. The choice can be overwhelming. When starting out it is sometimes easier to opt for those marked as 'reliable' or 'resilient'. However, I always look for comments on taste too. Often old-fashioned heritage varieties score well on this front, with modern plants bred more for storage durability or disease resilience. Each year I tend to grow a few trusted reliables alongside some new 'wild cards'.

Be warned – once you have had a few successes and realise the value a small packet can offer, buying seed can become a more serious addiction than a sweet tooth.

Saving Seeds

There was a time before seeds were sent by post or could be bought from our garden centres. Growers would choose the best mother plant and save its seed to ensure they could continue growing the following year. Once you start growing there is the option of participating in this practice – one that has been relied upon by previous generations.

Many plants will cross-pollinate so some seeds are easier to save than others. Tomatoes are a good place to start as tomato seeds can be relatively expensive to buy. Modern varieties rarely cross-pollinate so plants will be true to their mother plant and will taste the same, as long as they are not F1 type strains (check seed packet). For tips on seed saving The Real Seed Catalogue have excellent advice on their website (see resources section).

All seed should be stored in cool, dry and dark conditions. Temperatures should be kept reasonably steady. You are aiming to keep the seed dormant, as moisture, warmth and light will wake them up and they may start growing! I use paper bags or envelopes and keep them clearly labelled in a tin somewhere cool.

Planting Seeds

While it's true that different seed varieties require different growing conditions – slight variables in temperature and spacings (these details are given in Chapter 4) – the general method that I use remains roughly the same.

The planting methods below are the ones I follow for almost everything I grow.

The Direct Sowing Method

Direct sowing is where you plant seed straight into the ground. This way of sowing seeds is quicker but actually I rarely use it. On occasion, if I have a lovely fine tilth, the weather is good and my bed is pretty slug-free, I will sow some seeds straight out, but generally I find the module method, which we'll come to shortly, to be much more reliable.

To get started, simply rake over the surface to make sure the ground is weed free and the soil is fine enough for the seed to create good contact with it.

Use a piece of string held in place by sticks at either end to create a straight line along your bed. Then, using this as a guide, draw a straight line in the soil parallel to the string. I use the end of a garden tool or stick in order to do this. You are aiming to create a small trench in which to place your seed. This trench should be roughly twice the depth of the size of your seed.

Drop your seed along the line of the trench. Try to thin the seed out so it does not have too much competition from its bedfellows. Cover the seeds with some fine soil, pat down the line firmly and water in gently.

Tip

If the seeds are very small it can be useful to fold a piece of cardboard and pour seed into the fold. Gently tap the card as you move along the trench. This can help to give you a more even spacing.

The Cuttings Method

Some plants can easily be grown by taking cuttings from a mother plant. This works well when growing herbs as it can save time and expense. I always use this method for growing new rosemary plants, and often for sage.

Softwood cuttings (the new softer shoots that grow in spring) can be taken in spring, and semi-hardwood cuttings (shoots that have aged and turned woody) can be taken in summer.

Take your cuttings from the healthy, newer growth of your chosen plant and select non-flowering branches with plenty of leaves, roughly 10 cm in length (about 5–8 cm for thyme). I do this by pulling a small side-shooting branch downwards, away from the main stem. This should give you a 'heel' or strip of soft bark on your removed branch. Finally gently trim off the bottom third of leaves.

Plant your cutting straight out into a small pot of firmed-down freely draining compost, making sure that the bare stem – and not the leaves – are in the soil. I usually put two or three stems in each pot to increase my chances of success.

This is a quick and easy way of making new plants. Along the way I have had some failures but they have been far outweighed by success. Don't worry about being too technical – cuttings will often survive simply being bunged into a pot, watered and left on a sunny windowsill.

The Marvellous Module Method

Of all the tricks and techniques used to successfully grow plants, starting them somewhere protected in a module tray is my preferred method as it greatly increases the chances of success.

Thinking back to the basic conditions that plants need this makes perfect sense. If you begin by planting seed in trays you can easily give the seed and seedlings the optimum conditions required – food, water, light, heat and shelter – because they are portable.

Rather than open seed trays I nearly always use module trays. These are simply seed trays that are divided up into compartments. Unlike open seed trays, when transplanting out your seedlings you can plant the whole module into the ground without disturbing or pulling apart a plant's roots.

The types of module trays I use are generally A3-size trays with 150 holes (or plugs) for the seed compost and seed itself. I like this particular size tray but other similar kinds will work and there are lots of different types and sizes available from garden centres. In general I find a 2.5 cm diameter and depth of 5 cm provides enough space to give most smaller seeds a good start.

Working on a flat surface, pour seed compost over the tray and fill each hole then shake it down by banging the tray a few times on a hard surface. Then top up the tray with more compost, making sure the tray is full and the seed compost is firm and even. It is important there are no air pockets as the seeds need to have good contact with the soil in order to germinate.

Next make an indent with your finger, a stick or pencil, the depth of which should be approximately twice as deep as the size of seed you are planting. Some seeds like lettuce are so small they can sit just under the surface of the soil.

Sprinkle another thin layer of seed compost over the tray to cover the seed and gently pat it down. Again, you want the seed to be snugly in contact with the soil.

Finally, gently water the tray using a watering can or hose-head with a fine rose so the seeds are not displaced by the flow.

Tip

As a general rule I plant one seed per module hole. However, if you would like to keep plants small and tender – for things like salad leaves – place a few seeds in each module hole. Plant growth will be stunted by having to compete with fellow seedlings.

Where to Keep Your Seed Trays

With the basic plant requirements in mind, try and keep your module trays in a warm, light, sheltered place – ideally a greenhouse – and don't let the trays dry out. The seed compost will offer the seedling all the food (i.e. the nutrients) it requires for its early stages of growth.

Greenhouses are ideal for raising young plants in module trays. They are light, warm and protected from the elements and pests. If you don't have access to a greenhouse you can try and mimic greenhouse conditions as best you can.

For the last few years, from February onwards my bathroom has doubled up as a nursery for all of my most heat-hungry plants. I germinated 300-plus healthy tomato plants (plus all my cucumbers, courgettes and peppers) in there!

This is perhaps an extreme example; however, it does show what you can do with minimal resources and limited space. (My main issue now is not that I am in London, but that I have housemates!)

So, on a small scale, windowsills, conservatories or simple outdoor cold frames (a box with a glass or clear plastic lid like a mini-greenhouse) can be used to help nurture plants through their early stages. While indoor growing offers warmth and protection for plants from frosts, the main challenge is finding somewhere light enough to keep seedlings healthy after germination.

Seedlings will naturally bend towards the light source so you will need to turn them around or move them regularly as they grow. Ideally we would all have a little greenhouse to raise some of our food and maybe one day more people will. For now, if you don't have any suitable space available for plant raising – and if you don't want to fill your bathroom with seedlings – there is no shame in buying some young plants from a garden centre that have been raised by someone who does, though it will be more costly. 'Cut and come again' lettuces can offer especially good value.

Transferring Seeds to the Garden

There is another benefit to raising plants in module trays. Just before planting out you can give the bed they are being transferred to a quick final cultivation with a fork or rake. This creates a weed-free bed for the seedlings to go into. Your seedlings will have a head start on any weeds that come up later and increase their chances of outperforming the competition.

If you have raised plants indoors or in a greenhouse it's best to get them used to the colder outside temperatures

gradually. This is called 'hardening off'. First put your module trays outside on the morning of a warmish day. This will allow them to acclimatise before nightfall and even lower temperatures. Make sure that the area you place your module trays in is slug-free, and check it again when dark to be sure.

Once your seedlings have been outside for a few days they should be well adjusted enough to cope with being moved from the tray to the ground. Once your bed is ready, create a straight line in the ground. Unlike with seeds, I usually do this by eye but sometimes use string tied between two sticks and staked in the ground.

Make holes (I use a trowel or sometimes just my hands) for the module plants. To remove plants from a module tray gently push from underneath. Use a pencil or stick to push through the drainage hole. This helps to loosen the plant roots. If the plant module is not coming out easily, it can mean that the seedling needs to be left to grow a little longer so the root ball forms a secure bundle that will pull out neatly.

Once you have removed your plants, place one in each hole then gently firm them in, making sure they have good contact with the soil around them. A guide for how far apart they should be spaced is listed by individual vegetable in Chapter 4.

Finally, always water your plants in gently unless the rain saves you the job.

Mixed Planting

It may be easier to create order in a garden by planting the same crops side by side, but sometimes I like to experiment. And there's a reason for it. Raising complementary plants together can bypass the need for a strict rotation plan.

Through the very variety you create, you are achieving its goal – not to exhaust the same nutrients year after year. Mixing crops can give excellent results and fits in well with the principle of achieving balance in your system. It can also be a good way of making the most out of a small space.

In 2005 I worked on an organic farm on Vancouver Island, Canada. Here, Steven, a sensitive and practical farmer, showed me a system first used by the Mayans that used one crop's traits to benefit another. These were regarded as the 'three sisters' – courgettes, sweetcorn and beans. Established courgettes were planted first, offering ground cover to suppress weeds. We then planted sweetcorn at intervals between the courgette plants. The sweetcorn would rise tall above the courgette leaves, seeking out the large amounts of sunlight it required. Finally, a climbing bean seed would be planted at the base of the young, module-raised sweetcorn plant. As the bean germinated and grew, the sweetcorn would offer the support it needed to climb. Meanwhile the bean, being a legume, would benefit the soil by fixing nitrogen. The three plants together created a relationship of mutual benefit.

If you want to try mixed planting think about the eventual size, shape, height and depth of a vegetable in order to gauge what may work together. Plants need space to grow, so look at their shapes to make sure they will not be competing with one another in the same space above, and below ground.

Some plants are grown together for other reasons of mutual benefit. For example, the smell of onions may camouflage the position of another crop from predators like carrot fly.

A basic table of useful companion plants can be found on page 147 in the Side Shoots section.

In this chapter I have focused on 10 vegetables – or in some cases vegetable groupings – with certain qualities: those that offer many harvests, those that grow with ease and rapidity, those that offer you good value for space, and those that taste best when freshly picked.

I have included vegetables that have worked well for me but different things suit different people.

Be creative. My choices are just a way in.

So, here are my top 10 for beginners. Generally the easier they are to grow and the less space they occupy, the closer they will be to the top of the list.

1. Hardy herbs – sage, rosemary, thyme and marjoram
2. Tender herbs – parsley, basil, coriander, chervil and dill
3. Summer salads – lettuce, endives and chicories
4. Winter salads
5. Chard, perpetual spinach and true spinach
6. Beetroot
7. Courgettes and cucumbers
8. Tomatoes
9. Beans – French, runner and broad beans
10. Winter greens – kale and purple sprouting broccoli

1

Hardy (woody) Herbs
Sage, Rosemary, Thyme and Marjoram

One of my first jobs as a grower was to tend the herbs on a south-facing field in the heart of Somerset. I arrived knowing very little but over time learned about almost a hundred medicinal and culinary herbs. All of these herbs are steeped in folklore. For example, sage is traditionally meant to keep you young and fair, while rosemary symbolises remembrance. The intense flavour of all these herbs means that a little goes a long way in the kitchen.

Sage, rosemary and thyme can be planted reasonably densely to form areas that are both attractive and easy to manage. Lavender can be a nice addition to such areas. Their intoxicating smells attract bees and, equally, deter or confuse unwelcome visitors.

The beauty of these herbs is that they can be grown in the smallest of spaces. Even in individual pots, with the right conditions, the same plant can continue for many years.

Sowing Method

For rosemary use the cuttings method (see page 44).
For sage, thyme and marjoram, either use cuttings or, as
I prefer, sow from seed in module trays.
Conditions and timing: Sow under cover in early spring.

Planting Out

Timing: Mid spring, from May onwards.
Spacing: Rosemary 60–90 cm apart, sage 45–60 cm,
thyme and marjoram 25 cm.
*These, and the suggested spacings that follow, are
approximate measurements based on what has worked for
me in the past.*

Harvest

These versatile evergreens respond well to picking and in
spring and summer send up delicious, tender new growth.

Tips
— Woody herbs such as these like Mediterranean climes
  and thus prefer free-draining, sandier soils and sunny
  aspects.
— Taking cuttings as described earlier works well with
  lavender and other related plants.
— All of these woody herbs should be trimmed back
  after flowering. Just cut off any dead heads.
— Large rosemary twigs work well as perfumed
  barbecue skewers.

Trouble-shooting
— Woody herbs do age and eventually will need replacing
  if you want more tender offerings.

— While they grow well in pots, it is sensible to keep them separate from vegetable areas as herbs will stay in one place for a few years.
— Make sure they have free-draining soil and are not over-watered.
— Because of their Mediterranean origins, young plants may need shelter and protection.
— Though frost-hardy they will suffer if pruned before a freeze.

Soulmates

Rosemary: Lamb, roasted vegetables, soft cheeses, pasta.
Sage: Pork, risottos.
Thyme: Chicken, pork, roast potatoes.
Marjoram: Tomatoes, fish and meaty sauces.

THE HERB FIELD, MILVERTON

Three acres of medicinal plants to tend, harvest and propagate – this was my first job growing and I was completely inexperienced. The field was a quilt of vibrant colour, stripes of flowers, running across the red earth of a Somerset slope. It was where I first became intimate with individual plants, not knowing much about them technically, but getting to know their characters through touch and smell, from root to tip. The Herb Field Diaries – an intricate journal full of facts, stats and extraneous information compiled by my predecessors from seasons past – became my trusted friend.

It was satisfying work. In summer, with the blossom oils for tincture at their height, the volunteer 'WWOOFERs' (World Wide Opportunites on Organic Farms) and I would harvest bucket-loads of flowers: bright calendula, heavily scented Rosa rugosa and cheery red-oiled St John's wort. Then there were the endless species all with their own healing properties and names that hinted at the human relationship held within: comfrey, skullcap, feverfew, eyebright and sage.

Mallows, worts and sorrels to be chopped, macerated, dried or tinctured. The names reel off from memory: echinacea, iris, black cohosh, vervain, valerian, wormwood, southernwood, golden rod, arnica, chamomile, plantain, cleavers, dandelion,

hawthorn, yarrow, dock and nettle. The mysteriously exotic and the seemingly common weed suddenly given justification and worth.

When I think of that period it is the smells that return most acutely, cutting through time with ease. Heady valerian root, cleanly stabbing feverfew, smells so distinctive they became deeply etched in my memory.

We had an old tea cutting machine that looked like a relic from a Heath Robinson drawing. 'Bertha' had a massive wheel, razor-sharp, that would spin with a pleasant but sinister swish. The feeder would then stand on a platform, pushing in roots, leaf or flowers with refined judgement so the cog teeth pulled in the plant but not our fingers!

Harvesting roots required the most exertion, especially burdock that channelled deep into the hard subsoil of the earth and took a battle of wills to release. Once dug and washed in a cement mixer, all roots were spread over drying racks, glistening tentacles to be blanched by the sun. The plants took on their character and by the end of the summer they were as engrained in my mind as deeply as their scents were embedded in my palms.

2
Tender Herbs
Parsley, Basil, Coriander, Chervil and Dill

If I could only grow one herb I would choose parsley.
It is delicious, versatile, productive and grows nearly year
round when other tender herbs struggle with the cold.

Coriander can be left to flower. The green seeds from
the subsequent seed heads are delicious in cooking and
give an intense hit of perfumed coriander.

Sowing Method
Sow from seed in module trays.
Conditions and timing: For a continual harvest sow
successively in March, June and August so you have
crops towards winter. Keep last sowings under cover in a
greenhouse or equivalent.

Planting Out
Timing: After the last spring frosts when the young plants
have four or more leaves.

Spacing: For dill and basil 28 cm apart or in a pot of at least 28 cm in diameter, for others 15 cm apart.
Do not plant basil outside as it is likely to perish.
Instead 'grow on' under the protection of a greenhouse, conservatory or on a windowsill.

Harvest
Spring to autumn (parsley almost year round).

Tips
— For best results, sow chervil and coriander under cover slightly later, around August, as I find they bolt – i.e. switch from leaf production to flower and seed growth – from the summer heat when sown early.
— Chervil likes damp and shade.
— These herbs grow well in clumps and 2 to 5 seeds per module also works well. Bear in mind that the number of seeds sown together will affect leaf size.
— Regular weekly picking will help prolong their harvest; when harvesting basil, pick off the side shoots rather than mature leaves, as this will encourage new growth. Take care not to over-pick.
— These herbs are a good companion to grow next to tomatoes as the smell deters pests.

Trouble-shooting
— Tender herbs become easily stressed with too much heat or being transplanted. This can cause them to go to seed prematurely. If this happens cut the flower heads to extend their harvest.
— Eventually they will need regular re-sowings for a fresh crop (see Gardening Calendar at the end for guidelines).
— Parsley can be slow to germinate, but don't lose heart.

— An exotic plant like basil needs protection and heat.
It will perish quickly if it gets too cold. It also dislikes
being over-watered.

Soulmates

Dill: Fish, cucumber, sauerkraut, gherkins and
other pickles.

Chervil: Fish, torn into green salads.

Coriander: Carrot, curry, coconut milk, chilli.

Parsley: Staple foods like pasta, risotto and potatoes
(I use it with most meals).

Basil: Tomatoes, fish, olive oil, soft cheese.

3

Summer Salads
Lettuce, Endives and Chicories

Salads are easy to grow. In order to cover the season it is essential to keep sowing seeds successively at certain points throughout the year. This way you can have salad leaves almost continually.

Sowing Method
From seed in module trays, but can be sown directly. Just make sure you thin them out.

Conditions and timing:
Lettuce: Start off under cover from late January then successively in mid March, late May, July and September to cover the season.

Endives and chicory: Start off under cover from May to mid August. Early to mid July sowings give best results.

Planting Out
Timing: From March.
Spacing: 25 cm apart.

Harvest
Lettuce: May to winter (if under cover). Best results are from seed sown through spring for harvest up until early July.
Endives and chicory: At their best from late summer through to early October.

Tips
— The life span of a lettuce can be prolonged by regularly picking outer leaves and pinching out any flowering stems. In this way a single plant can give you a substantial harvest for up to three months!
— There are many types of salad leaf varieties to cover the summer period. The most yielding by far is lettuce.
— Lettuces thrive in the bright but not too hot conditions of spring. By mid June lettuce should be abundant, so whole heads can be harvested. Even then it will continue sending up leaves from its old stump.
— Endives and chicories are best sown from late June. After the June Solstice light levels and heat diminish which means they are less likely to bolt, and will produce leaf rather than try to flower.
— Regular harvesting helps keep air flowing between plants.

Trouble-shooting
— If conditions are too hot, lettuce seed will not germinate. If the weather is warm, try keeping seed trays outside.

- Lettuce will bolt if it is too hot so in summer it's best planted in areas that are not in direct sun all day.
- Lettuce requires lots of water. In dry summers, regular watering can also help prevent root aphids from killing the plants.
- Slugs love lettuce and are the main pest, so try and water in the morning to restrict their activity (see page 98 for more slug advice).
- Mildew can be a problem in warm, wet conditions. Regular harvesting helps keep air flowing between plants.

Soulmates

Lettuce has few culinary foes and goes with almost anything.
Endives and chicory: goats' cheese, orange, pork and fish.

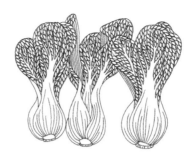

4

Winter Salads

Brassicas: Rocket, land cress, red Russian kale, mizuna, mibuna, pak choi, tatsoi and mustards

Others: Claytonia (or winter purslane), lamb's lettuce, endives, chicories and radicchios

———

August is the month of transition for salads. Summer lettuce begins to diminish and conditions become much more suited to the peppery and oriental leaves of winter salads – some of my favourite leaves of the year.

From August you need to be ready to sow your winter salad seeds. Their hardy and tasty leaves will provide harvest from autumn right through to early spring. Growth will naturally slow down, as light fades and temperatures fall. However, the plants are great survivors. When I worked at Hugh Fearnley-Whittingstall's River Cottage we planted them outside, rather than raising them in a greenhouse, and were able to gently pick their leaves through the autumn to early winter.

These leaves are intense, bitter and peppery in flavour and full of vitality, offering a winter boost just when you need it.

Sowing Method
From seed in module trays.
Conditions and timing: Sow under cover from July to September.

Planting Out
Timing: Preferably under cover in a greenhouse from August.
Spacing: 22 cm apart.

Harvest
From September through to the following spring.

Tips
— These kinds of leaves grow well in containers, which can be moved to any freed-up space in a greenhouse over winter.
— To keep these winter leaves healthy and productive they need to be regularly picked by taking their larger outer leaves.
— If planting outside, offer some protection from the extreme cold of winter with horticultural fleece or bubblewrap. Winter salads are hardy within reason and will yield more return if given some protection from the cold.
— From March they will continue to grow steadily until the increasing light levels finally give them the signal to bolt and flower.

— Follow the final harvest with a dressing of compost and then plant out summer greenhouse crops such as tomatoes or cucumbers in their place.

— Larger leaves of mizuna, mibuna, tatsoi or bulbs of pak choi are delicious to eat as a steamed green. Ginger, garlic and soy complement them very well.

Trouble-shooting

— Brassica salad leaves will be struck down with flea beetle if grown too early. I don't sow them before late July.

— I tend to sow most brassicas around the beginning of September, planting them out in a greenhouse once my tomatoes and summer crops have finished.

— Growth will slow down from November until March and the quantity of leaves produced will reduce.

— Ideally leave a four-year gap before planting any brassicas again in the same ground, otherwise pervasive disease may occur.

Soulmates

Rocket and land cress: pizza, pasta, olive oil, salt, cold meats, most cheeses.

Mizuna, mibuna, pak choi and tatsoi: broths, noodle soups, white meats.

All of these leaves go beautifully together raw, dressed in a salad.

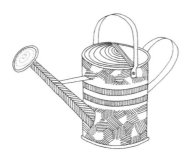

5

Chard, Perpetual Spinach and True Spinach

These plants are useful as they have a very long season. Chard is one of the most valuable plants to grow for a consistent and abundant supply of tasty greens.

Perpetual spinach is actually a type of leaf beet that shares more characteristics with chard than it does with true spinach. Taste-wise it can supplement true spinach well, especially when cooked. It is also easier to grow as it is less tender and does not bolt as rapidly.

As the weather gets colder growth will slow and the plant's roots are eventually killed off. However, in milder years, I have found that these plants can survive over winter to give a month or two of harvest again in early spring. Growth of the same plant will begin again in spring as soil temperatures rise.

True spinach grows rapidly in spring and early summer. Its leaves are more tender and less acidic than perpetual spinach and chard so even larger leaves can be added to salads. However, younger leaves are often best, especially for eating raw in salads. They are not only prettier but also more tender and tasty. It is the most sensitive of the three and thus the trickiest to grow.

Sowing Method
From seed in module trays or sow directly into soil.
Conditions and timing:
Chard and Perpetual Spinach: Under cover from March. Sow successively in June and August to cover the season.
True spinach: Under cover from February. Sow successively in April and July to mid August (avoid May and June sowings as it is sensitive to heat and is likely to bolt).

Planting Out
Timing: From March to October.
Spacing: For baby spinach as salad leaves from 10 cm. For large plants 28 cm.

Harvest
April to October (longer if under cover).

Tips
— March sowings will start to flower from June. Replace with a fresh crop that you have started in modules in May. Alternatively keep picking out the flowers, but new plants will be more tender to eat.
— With all varieties, for smaller salad leaves put up to four seeds in each module and grow plants closer together.
— Chard can survive frosts right through winter, providing you with some precious greens even until the following May, so you can sow as late as September.

- At some point the plants will show signs of flowering. You can encourage further leaf growth by pinching out flowering stems.
- Keeping roots moist and regularly picking the leaves will delay the process of the plant creating seed over leaf.
- Pick young leaves by hand or knife. If cutting across the plant with a knife be sure to leave the smallest new leaves at the base to replace the growth. Picking by hand encourages leaf re-growth faster than if you cut plants with a knife.
- August sowings of true spinach can provide useful winter salad leaves but this will depend on how cold the soil becomes.

Trouble-shooting

- Slugs, birds and even woodlice can all make a meal of more tender leaves. To increase the plants' chances of survival start them off in the protected walls of module trays.
- True spinach is more heat-sensitive and prone to bolt. As a result it will have a shorter season and give best results when conditions are not too hot.

Soulmates

Butter, garlic, puy lentils, olive oil, salt.

6

Beetroot

Beetroot are easy to grow, have a long season and offer sweet and earthy flavours. They are rich in vitamin A and delicious eaten small – about the size of a golf ball. Cutting beetroot before cooking allows precious flavour to be lost, whereas roasting them whole helps to emphasise their sweetness. Small beetroot leaves make a pretty salad. Larger leaves can be cooked like spinach.

Shops tend to limit their beetroot offering to the traditional dark-purple variety, when in actual fact a kaleidoscope of candy-coloured varieties are available: gold, ruby, and the most beautiful variety, Chioggia. It has delicate layers of pink and white, with each ring reflecting a lunar month from its first growth.

Like most root vegetables, beetroot can be stored for many months once harvested. Traditionally they were packed in boxes of straw and left in cellars. Anywhere with similar dark, cool conditions to those underground will allow an extended life. The easiest way to do this is to leave them in the ground, unless frosts become severe.

Sowing Method

From seed in module trays (one seed per hole) or sow directly into soil.

Conditions and timing: Under cover from March to early July. Succession sow in May and early July.

Planting Out

Timing: Every few weeks from April to July to give continual harvest.

Spacing: 8 cm apart.

Harvest

July to February – depending on sowing times.

Tips

— I grow beetroot in modules (one seed per hole), planting them out in rows approx. 8 cm apart from April. This ensures even spacing and root size.
  If direct sowing, the space between the beetroot will affect their size but you can thin out as you harvest.
— Planting extra in July will allow you to keep some in over winter, offering fresh leaf in spring.

Trouble-shooting

— Beetroot tend to bolt, going to seed and leaving the roots inedible. Try bolt-resistant varieties such as Boltardy.
— Leaves are prone to being nipped by birds; however, the roots are usually hardy enough to sustain this. If you have severe bird trouble, cover the beetroot with nets or put up bird scarers.

Soulmates

Cumin, crème fraiche, balsamic vinegar, yoghurt.

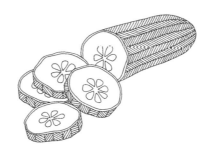

7

Courgettes and Cucumbers

Courgettes

I have a love for courgette plants. With their large Gauginlike leaves they offer good weed cover and are quick and easy to grow. Their only difficulty is the kind of problem I like: managing to eat them all.

I always grow a few varieties offering yellow, striped and the traditional sleek dark green. Courgette plants can use up a fair amount of space but they are definitely worth it!

Try the fruit at different sizes. They will have a firmer texture when small. If picked late, they become large and can be cooked like marrows, stuffed or made into marrow and ginger jam or chutney.

Courgettes, and indeed all of the Cucurbitae family, produce wonderful, edible flowers. Fragile and beautiful, they perish to the touch so it is rare to find them for sale. They simply would not survive the supermarket regime. Courgette flowers are lovely stuffed and deep-fried or simply torn into salads for colour and their delicate flavour.

Sowing Method

Sow in pots of approx. 30 cm in diameter (or large enough to take at least two handfuls of potting compost).
Conditions and timing: Under cover from April to early June.

Planting Out

Timing: From mid May.
Spacing: approx. 70 cm apart.

Harvest

June to early October.

Tips

— Sow seeds so they sit vertically in the soil. This reduces the chance of them rotting before germination.
— If planted out in May, plants will be helped by a cover of horticultural fleece, especially if it is particularly cold.

Trouble-shooting

— From August, leaves may suffer from mildew. Don't worry, as they will continue to produce fruit but if severe simply prune affected leaves.
— Though hardy, these are exotic plants that do not like the cold. Production will slow and they will be killed after the first autumnal frosts. Leave in as ground cover that will break down over winter.
— Once planted out I undersow plants with green manures such as white clover or trefoil, see page 147. Simply scatter seed over the area, water and firm in.

Soulmates

Olive oil, salt, pepper, goats' cheese, basil, garlic.

Cucumbers

Cucumbers are part of the same family as courgettes so can be raised in a similar way. They are, like courgettes, exotic plants and need warmth to germinate and survive. They like sheltered, moist conditions so do best under cover – ideally in a greenhouse. If this isn't an option, make sure you choose an outdoor variety.

Cucumbers are prolific and produce large amounts of fruit from a few plants. They are a good source of vitamin C and other beneficial minerals when eaten fresh. Cucumber pickle is absolutely delicious and versatile, good with cheese, meats and fish (see recipe on page 116).

GROWER'S TOP 10

Tips

— Fruits are mainly made up of water so require lots while growing! Increase how much you water as the season goes on.
— Vining varieties can grow very tall so will need canes or strings to grow up for support. If they reach its top, they can be trained back down.
— When buying seed try to obtain indoor, all-female, hybrid F1 varieties for the most consistent yields.
— Check all chosen varieties are female. If not, remove male flowers (those without fruit), because if female flowers are pollinated the resulting fruit will be bitter.
— Cucumber stems are brittle so may break easily.
— Be especially careful when picking fruit so you don't damage the plant. I find it best to use a knife.
— If cucumbers get too large they will be tough, but can still be peeled or pickled.
— Outdoor cucumbers have tougher, bumpier skin and are also good pickled.
— Dill makes a good companion plant to repel red spider mites, which are prone to attack cucumbers.

Trouble-shooting

— Cucumbers are vulnerable to slugs when small but starting off under cover should offer protection.

— By late summer mildew tends to coat the underneath of larger leaves. Remove such leaves and plants will usually continue to bear fruit.

— Chopped comfrey leaves mixed with water and left for a few weeks make a potash-rich 'tea' that can be diluted and watered in to give plants a boost.

— Yellowing of lower leaves and tiny cobwebs are a sign of red spider mite. If it does get established, buy phytoseiulus (another mite that preys on the red spider mite).

— Cucumbers and all squash can be undersown with white clover or trefoil, see page 147.

Soulmates

Dill, salt, pepper, olive oil, feta, vinegars, yoghurt, mint.

8

Tomatoes

On a wintry February morning, I planted some golden seeds in compost and put them in my small bathroom. We shared this living space for months. It wasn't until late July that I was able to reap the fruits of my labour, however, the months of patient watching and waiting were worth that first taste.

Tomatoes require a great deal of nurturing but, in return, you are hugely rewarded for your efforts. A sun-warmed tomato, the smell of the leaf, the greeny-black resin that coats your fingers when pruning, the satisfaction of pinching out virile side shoots that appear from nowhere – I love the whole process, right down to salvaging the last green tomato and, with some reluctance, pulling up plants to make way for winter salads.

There are climbing, bush and dwarf varieties. Often the most delicious varieties are not grown commercially because of their small yield or fragile nature. When growing at home you have more freedom to experiment.

Sowing Method

Sow seeds in module trays.

Conditions and timing: Under cover, February to March.

Planting Out

After four or five weeks, when the plants have about four leaves and before the stems become long and flimsy, they can be gently re-potted into pots of approx. 10 cm diameter. When they reach about 20 cm and have a few flowers beginning to open, plant out in a sheltered and sunny position.

Timing: April to June.

Spacing: approx. 55 cm apart.

Harvest

July to October.

Tips

— Tomatoes are exotic plants from South America. They don't like the cold, so start seeds off in late winter under gentle heat of about 20 degrees. Houses generally offer this continual source of warmth, though make sure light is available.
— First growth is very slow. Be patient.
— When re-planting, leave a gap of approx. 5 mm of stem between the lower leaves and soil. The rest of the stem can be under the soil as tomatoes like to be planted deep.
— Provide some support; this is especially needed for the cordon variety. Canes can be used or, if you have a structure on which to tie it, a strong piece of string can be loosely noosed around the bottom or buried under the root ball when you plant out. Tie the top of the

string to whatever structure – such as a wire, or poly-tunnel bar – you may have above. As they grow, plants can be twisted around the string or tied to canes, to help them train themselves upwards.

— Side shoots will appear between the stem and main leaf all through the season. Gently snap these out. The same goes for any shoots growing at the end of trusses (a fruit-bearing branch). Such growth will waste valuable energy and slow their fruiting. It will also create more shade and prevent air circulation, in turn increasing the chances of disease.

— With outdoor plants cut out the top of the plant when they have at least six trusses to save energy for fruit. I tend to remove the first lowest truss of flowers as otherwise it attracts slugs and gets damaged by dragging on the ground. You can also remove extra leaf, but remember what you are trying to achieve – a balance between having enough leaf for the plant to photosynthesise but also allowing in sun and air. You can experiment a bit with this as tomato plants can handle quite rigorous pruning.

— The key to success lies with the soil. Spread a layer of compost or well-rotted manure before or just after planting out. Tomatoes need a fertile soil that will easily hold moisture.

— Seaweed or comfrey tea is an extra source of potash for the plants. I grow a patch of comfrey which I let break down in a barrel of rainwater before diluting and pouring around the base of each plant. Using lots of compost can bypass the need to give tomato plants any supplementary feeds.

— Under-watering will decrease yield but intensify flavour. Over-watering can result in split tomatoes. Try and find the right balance.

— With first frost pick any unripe tomatoes, and put on a sunny windowsill or in a sealed plastic container. The ethylene they give off should help them to ripen.
— If you are not growing tomatoes in a greenhouse, be sure to get outdoor varieties and put them in your warmest, most sheltered spot. Against a south-facing wall is ideal. Use a grow bag if necessary, as warmth is essential.
— By the autumn, light levels and warmth will decrease. To help plants use their failing resources most efficiently simply pinch out the tops of all plants. Also water less often.
— Tomatoes can be undersown with white clover or trefoil, see page 147.

Trouble-shooting

— Blight, also affecting potatoes, is the biggest vulnerability for tomatoes. It is an airborne fungal disease thriving in warm, damp conditions. Leaves and fruit will develop brown marks. Make sure plants are watered at their root so as not to make the leaves damp. Blight remains in the soil so don't compost affected plants and be sure to grow new season's plants in a new place.
— Companion planting with tagetes (Chinese marigolds) can help deter whitefly as they hate the smell, see page 147. Basil will also draw aphids away from your prize crop.

Soulmates

Olive oil, basil, soft cheese, sage, French tarragon, olives, balsamic vinegar, salt and pepper.

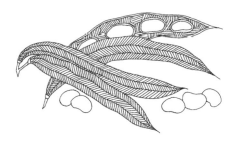

9

Beans

French Beans, Runner Beans and Broad Beans

French and Runner Beans

French and runner beans are grown in much the same way. Though runners are a bit more hardy, if I could choose only one variety, it would be the French bean.
They are quick to grow, high-yielding and delicious.

As well as the traditional green varieties, you can source purple and yellow ones which are equally tasty. Adding a little sugar in the cooking water will help purple beans keep their vibrant colour when cooked.

All beans are tastiest when young, from the moment they snap when bent. When picking French and runner beans be careful not to damage the plants – they are not always willing to release their bounty.

If you have limited space, use the height of French and runner beans to your advantage by using the space left on the ground to grow other vegetables (see

Companion Plants, page 147). Here I have experimented with courgettes, sweetcorn, onions and carrots. Courgettes work particularly well because they are low-growing and can still flourish despite the slight shading of beans. Mixed planting such as this also prevents weeds growing in otherwise bare ground. When mixing vegetables remember to think about their physicality in the space, in other words their depth, height and spread of leaf.

When planting out, remember that beans love the sun but the taller varieties will require some shelter as they are more vulnerable to being blown over by the wind.

At the end of the season, if you'd like to save seeds, leave some beans on the plant as it dies then remove the pod and store somewhere cool and dry for next year.

Sowing Method
Start off in pots of approx. 10 cm diameter.
Conditions and timing: Under cover from March to July. Succession sow every six weeks to cover the season.

Planting Out
A month after sowing, when plants are a few centimetres tall. Wait until after the last frosts seem to have passed.
Timing: May to June (slightly earlier if under cover, protected from frost).
Spacing: approx. 20 cm apart, further if adding pyramids.

Harvest
From mid June to October depending on sowing times.

Tips

— Climbing beans will need support from canes or strings. Triangular 'pyramid' structures are an easy, strong and attractive way of doing this.

— To see if beans are ready, try bending them in the middle. If they are not ready to be picked, they will not break.

— The more you pick the beans, the more they will yield.

— The flowers are also edible!

— Runner beans can be grown in the same way as French beans. Unlike self-pollinating beans, they need to be pollinated. Plant them in a sheltered spot to help attract bees to their flowers and protect them from being blown over.

— Dry some of your beans out on paper to give you new seeds for the following year.

— Beans can be undersown with white clover and trefoil, see page 147.

— Runner beans and broad beans are hardier than French beans, so are easier to grow outside.

- Slugs will devour them when young (see slug advice, page 98). Starting them off under cover helps to protect them when they are most vulnerable.
- They are prone to attacks of aphid – who love the young pods – and blackfly. To remedy this plant some nasturtiums or tagete (Chinese marigold) flowers alongside. These 'companion plants' will attract aphid-eating ladybirds, lacewings and hoverflies – and create the diversity needed for a healthy, balanced environment.
- Protect with horticultural fleece during sudden cold spells.
- Halo blight (spots on the leaves) is often carried in the seed but the damage is mainly cosmetic.
- If not harvested regularly, beans can become tough.

Soulmates

See page 87.

GROWER'S TOP 10

Broad Beans

In northern climes such as Norway, gluts of broad beans are often dried and made into a simple paste during winter. The smaller varieties are rarely found in shops and, though they require more work for less quantity, they offer a unique sweet taste of springtime. Your pinched-out tops can also be delicious as a steamed delicacy.

Sowing Method
Start off in pots of approx. 10 cm in diameter, or sow directly into soil.
Conditions and timing: Direct sow mid November or under cover from late February to May. Succession sow every three weeks to give a continual harvest.

Planting Out
Timing: April to June.
Spacing: 20 cm apart in rows approx. 60 cm apart.

Harvest
April to September.
Note: *If you wish for a slightly earlier harvest, around April, broad beans can be sown in November. However, having them in the ground over winter can increase their vulnerability to rotting or being eaten by birds and mice.*

Tips

— Pinching out the top few centimetres of growth on the main stems after the first pods appear and flowers begin to wilt allows energy to be focused on new pods.
— To harvest, pull bean downwards away from the stem.
— Being of the legume family, bean plants help fix some nitrogen into the soil. When removing plants after they have stopped yielding, try to leave the roots in the soil where they will add fertility.

Trouble-shooting

— Chocolate spot is a disease that may leave marks or holes on the leaf but such damage is mainly cosmetic. Plants put under stress through lack of space or drought will be weaker and therefore more susceptible.
— Blackfly can attack broad bean plants. If caught early they can be wiped off. I remove more serious attacks simply by spraying with the hose pipe. Pinching out the top of the plants once they have flowered removes the blackflies' favourite place to inhabit and does not damage plants. Blackfly is often a symptom of plants that are under stress. This is usually caused by either drought or lack of organic matter in the soil so keep beans watered and make sure soils are topped up with lots of compost. Sowing seeds in the autumn also decreases the chances of blackfly attacks.

Soulmates for French, Runner and Broad Beans

Lemon juice, olive oil, parsley, garlic, salt, pork.

10

Winter Greens
Kale and Purple Sprouting Broccoli

No vegetable is more sleek than cavolo nero, sometimes called Italian kale. Long lines of it would stretch before us far up the Coleshill vegetable field, statuesque and handsome, glistening kings of the morning frost. Kale is easy to grow, frost-hardy, and available in many varieties, flavours, shapes and colours.

Purple sprouting broccoli is one of the most delicious things on the planet. I only came across it after I started working on organic farms, and in the fields I would graze my way down the lines as I harvested.

You can buy it in supermarkets now but I find that the taste is compromised when it's not fresh, so this is a good one to try and grow yourself.

It is delicious cooked simply but when combined with hollandaise sauce it becomes sublime.

Sowing Method

Sow seeds in module trays.
Conditions and timing: Under cover mid June to early July.

Planting Out

Timing: Late July to late August (depending on variety).
Spacing: approx. 50 cm apart.

Harvest

Kale: From September to April.
Purple sprouting broccoli: From November to May.

Tips – Kale

— Kale can be sown before the suggested date but watch out for caterpillars. I plant mine out around mid August.
— Leaves are much better eaten after a frost as they are more tender.
— Green kales tend to be more productive but reds seem less afflicted by pests.

Tips – Purple sprouting broccoli

— There are early, mid and late varieties so try to grow a range to cover the season.

Trouble-shooting

— Autumn caterpillars and birds can cause problems as food is sparse at this time of year. Caterpillars can be picked off by hand. For greater protection lay a net over stakes above young plants.

Soulmates

Kale: Pork, butter, rosemary, anchovies and garlic.
Broccoli: Butter, hollandaise sauce.

COLESHILL

Arriving at Swindon bus station was not the most hopeful of new beginnings. However, after being picked up by Pete, my new grower mentor, I arrived in Coleshill, a small village perched between the Vale of the White Horse and the Cotswolds. Here, on my first night, I found many of its inhabitants enjoying a few drinks in the local pub.

Coleshill Organics consisted of a 6-acre walled garden, another 23-acre field, nine poly-tunnels, and its team of growers: Pete, Sonia, Anthony, and now me and Will Johnson, the young apprentices.

I asked Will to recollect what those two years we shared had meant to him and it so mirrored how I felt: 'I can't say that I decided to make a career out of veg growing in some profound moment of clarity. I was 24 and realised I'd spent the last 18 months volunteering and WWOOFing on farms and might as well get a paid job. The only one I saw advertised was near Swindon (I'd heard of their football team) and a few weeks later I moved into a caravan inside the walled garden of Coleshill National Trust Estate.

At Coleshill I literally learned by doing. Rather than seeing my physical labour as relentless drudgery, I enjoyed the process of becoming a human machine, a proverbial workhorse; building stamina and strength and work ethic week by week, month by month. I revelled in the news that I was a much more renewable energy source than fossil fuels.

Each autumn we would take the mesh off the brassica plot and reveal a half-acre collage of red, green and purple; a picture of life when all else in the field was dying, hibernating or was safely tucked up in a storeroom. It would be in a different place each year and you'd have to go to the top of the hill to see it properly: it was like unveiling a huge work of art.

Pete was a good person to learn small-scale veg growing from because he was passionate about his work and an assertive leader who drove the team to achieve a superhuman amount of work each day. I can't deny that like most people who've never actually done it, I'd imagined 'growing' as quite a romantic, laid-back, stress-free kind of thing to do for a living. I still think of it as romantic, but I stopped seeing it as a laid-back option when I started working for Pete. And as someone who now manages the veg growing on a piece of land, I can fully appreciate why.

That said, I could see even with all his years of experience that Pete still enjoyed the beautiful side of growing; I remember him pointing to a crop of phacelia and telling me to look closely. When you look closely at a flowering phacelia crop you will see a bee on nearly every flower of every plant.'

Our time working at Coleshill was a period of very hard work to create a big beautiful garden. The brassica collage that moved around the field, the phacelia crop that improved the environment above and below the soil – these images have become visual reminders of the theories and practices that we were there to learn. There's nothing like eating food (lots of it!) that you have worked hard to produce. And there's nothing like the head space and peace of mind that can be found in being a labourer on a small organic farm.

Edible Flowers

And finally, when growing vegetables I always grow flowers. Sometimes the flowers can threaten to overwhelm the other crops, but I try to keep my flower passion in check. As a compromise, I generally grow lots of edible flowers as they are so beautiful and useful. Nasturtiums – I have discovered – love a warm, damp climate. A summer in Wales can create vast jungles of beautiful leaf and flower.

There is no denying they are pretty, but they are also good for the whole system. Pollinators love them, pests love them (tempting them away from your valuable crops) ... and I love them.

Growing Edible Flowers

Calendula, borage and nasturtiums – sow March to July. Grow in modules or put single seeds straight into the ground. I like all these flowers at either end of my raised beds. To harvest, gently pick the flower head.

After one year's sowings I have found that all three have self-seeded the following year. I let them come up and if they are somewhere I don't want them, once they have a few leaves I move them to the end of the beds.

The flowers from mizuna, rocket, fennel, dill, chives, coriander, courgette and other squash can all be used to brighten up any meal.

My Edible Flower Salads

My summer salads are brought to life by adding a variety of edible flowers.

The following flower heads can all be used to add taste, texture and colour, and as a garnish for other dishes. Such delicacies need to be picked and used fresh, so won't be found in the shops, but can occasionally be spotted at farmers' markets. Generally they are simply too good to be bought and sold.

I use the following:

— Borage flowers: I have been told this flower helps to boost serotonin – it definitely makes me happy. Borage is also lovely in a big jug of Pimm's.
— Calendula / marigold: Pull petals off a flower head and disperse through salads. Their bright orange and yellow hues warm the spirit, and for the body they are meant to be a good hormone balancer.
— Nasturtium: Tear nasturtium flowers, and add their smaller leaves, for a hit of hot peppery flavour.
— Gently torn courgette and squash flowers.
— Small golden heads of fennel flowers.
— A pinch of rocket blossom or yellow mizuna flowers.

5
Keep Watch

As your plants grow, the physical work may slow down but now is the time to use your powers of observation. It's a wild world out there and nature is unpredictable. While we cannot control the weather or unforeseen pest invasion we can keep a gentle eye on things and try to predict or remedy any potential threat to our precious plants.

Common Problems

Slugs

Slugs are by far the most troublesome garden pest and the downfall of many growers. Using module trays rather than direct sowing can offer some protection to the vulnerable seedling during their first few weeks.

Slugs like damp, dark conditions. It is therefore a good idea not to position your beds next to such habitats, e.g. grass or mulches. Slugs do not like crawling over dry or sharp material. Spreading things like wood chip or egg shell near the base of your plants can deter them.

Watering your plants in the evenings can aid and

encourage slug movement as they like to travel when conditions are moist. You may have noticed all the slug trails around first thing in the morning, as they are most active at night. Try and water early in the mornings to help reduce night-time slug activity around your plants.

Surprisingly slugs have a good sense of smell and will smell their way back to their (and your!) favourite plants. The good news is that this sense of smell can be turned to your advantage. I have found beer traps (low, easily accessible containers of beer) to be a successful way of drawing slugs away from crops. Slugs are greatly attracted to the yeast in beer and will slither in to a merry death.

There are many other options to combat slugs, from slug pellets to copper tape. I find these expensive so prefer other means. One of the most simple and effective is to go out at night with a torch and collect them.

In moments of slug despair when all else has failed, I try to remember they are good for the birds.

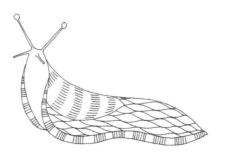

Weeds

At some point, out of nowhere, weeds begin to appear.
Try to catch them as soon as possible by gently running
your hands between rows of plants, brushing away
unwanted seedlings. I have learned the hard way that this
prompt action can save a lot of time and effort later on.
If weeds do get out of hand (and sometimes they just do)
try to pull them before they flower and spread their seed.

Weeds can be composted but if they have started to
produce seed or are persistent (like couch grass, nettle,
dock and dandelion) keep them separate. I put them in a big
water-filled bucket or an old black compost sack. When they
become unrecognisable add them to the compost heap.

Despite various battles over the years, I have come
to the conclusion that weeds are not the enemy. Weed
banks can be a wonderful source of food and habitat –
just not for us. Weeds can even be useful. Nettle leaves
make a nitrogen-rich 'compost tea' if put in a bucket with
water, while dead stems are an excellent home for helpful
predators. Chickweed can lead us to fertile soil, and
buttercups indicate waterlogging, signalling what's going
on below ground. In such situations weeds gain elevated
titles: 'medicinal herbs', 'compost tea', or 'soil indicators'.
So it becomes a question of perspective.

I avoid commercial weedkillers as they pollute soil and
water courses, which is not good for anyone. In practice,
looking after ourselves cannot be separated from caring
for the whole environment.

The Weather and Your Soil

The more I grow things the more I have become obsessed
with the weather. This is probably because to a large

degree weather governs the work you will have to do for your crops. With heat, frost, wind and rain, jobs on the land can change faster than a summer's day in Wales.

I try to cheerfully accept it and enjoy my lack of control – this is fine when I get things right. It takes some failures to develop a sixth sense for your plants – when they will need protection, support or a drink. It takes a bit of time but it is a good feeling to have something to connect you back to the elements.

With any cultivation you need to think about protecting the structure of your soil. The structure of your soil dictates whether water can first be absorbed into it, and then retained by it. A better structure allows the soil to conserve this precious resource more easily.

Try to be aware of your soil's water content. Too wet and you will compact the soil; too dry and you will expose the surface area to the elements, allowing evaporation of valuable moisture.

Use your common sense. Trust your instincts.

Protect the Soil

Bare soil created in order to plant seeds or seedlings is actually soil in an unnatural state. You generally do not find bare soil in the wild. It is soil at its most vulnerable, as its natural defences against sun, wind, rain and compaction have been stripped away. This is the state where the soil fertility can easily be washed away, causing pollution to our rivers. The fertility, so useful in our soils, causes an imbalance in our rivers. Algae thrives and consequentially oxygen is sapped away, along with other river life.

Green manures and mulches can help guard against such fertility loss and soil damage.

It is important to work your soil when it's not too wet or dry to try to minimise the damage you do to it, mainly through compaction. Soil takes years to create and hours to destroy, so protecting it from erosion and preserving it for future generations is important.

Keeping Soil Fertile

One of the main difficulties in horticulture is how to maintain soil fertility, keeping the high levels of nitrogen that all plants require for growth. Conventional agriculture relies upon the use of manufactured nitrogen which is extracted using vast amounts of fossil fuel energy and water to produce man-made fertiliser. This process in turn releases nitrous oxide into the atmosphere which further contributes to climate change. This is the fertility source that currently underpins our whole system of food production.

The trouble with this system is that it does not address the wider picture of soil health. It is a system of dependency, reliant upon readily available yet finite resources. The quantity and affordability of the food on our plate is subject to the fluctuations in the price and availability of fossil fuels.

This system is also based on a short-term reliance on something that is limited in supply and thus becoming increasingly expensive. It seems to me rather irrational to base the majority of our food production on a system that will only work for a reasonably short period of time, especially when we have other options. Sustainable, long-term systems, such as using nitrogen-fixing green manures, maintain soil fertility while looking at the bigger picture of soil health – without a reliance upon resources and earth capital that will eventually, and inevitably, dry up.

How to Boost Your Soil's Fertility Organically

For growers, the difficulty often comes down to sourcing enough fertility to match what you take away from the soil in yield or what is leached away by the elements.

As discussed earlier, compost offers a brilliant way to cycle waste, transforming it into rich humus that will feed plants, give structure to the soil and help retain water. The main difficulty with compost is finding enough. To make compost you need a source of organic matter, but if you don't have much household waste and only have a small garden there are other sources that it is possible to tap into.

When attempting to set up a garden of raised beds on her London housing estate, my sister Barley rang her council. She managed to source 15 tonnes of compost for free, but had no idea what 15 tonnes looked like. When it was delivered and deposited on the pavement outside, her neighbours were – perhaps justifiably – unimpressed. In panic she used the internet site 'Freecycle' to tell people it was there to collect for no cost. Over the next week a stream of local people emerged with barrows, vans and sacks. Her experience highlighted that one person's rubbish can become another person's gain. It is a question of perceived value. Composted organic matter can be found, and sometimes in bulk and for free!

Animal Magic

Animal muck is a really strong source of fertility for the garden. A good source are livery stables, where manure is often seen as a waste product so is free to collect. It needs to be broken down and composted well before you put it on your bed, but it can help speed up the composting process if mixed in with your heap. The presence of bright pink brandling worms indicate it is ready to use. If less well rotted you can put a layer at the bottom of your raised bed as a base layer. Here it will add some warmth and gradually break down. Poultry manure is another rich source of nitrogen. Mixing chicken muck or diluted urine with your compost will also benefit your heap.

Mulches

A mulch is something you use to cover soil at different times of the year for an array of reasons. Some mulches are organic (e.g. compost or straw) and some are man-made (e.g. Mypex plastic woven ground cover, or cardboard). In spring a mulch can be used to keep a bed weed-free and ready for planting, while summer mulches may be used as tools to retain moisture and suppress weeds. Autumn and winter mulches such as green manure (see also page 35) are perhaps the most important, as these help to protect soil from erosion over the winter months and can also help store and add fertility for the following year.

Green Manures

A green manure is a plant that is sown to improve a soil's health or boost its fertility.

Any plants in the legume family (from beans to clover) have the remarkable ability to fix the nitrogen from the air onto their roots in a form that is accessible to other plants. This is a sustainable form of acquiring nitrogen that by-passes the need to use man-made fertilisers.

All green manures can be used to cover the ground to protect it from the elements and prevent nutrients leaching away. Instead nutrients will be held in the green manure crop which is turned into the soil in spring or summer. Nutrients are thus cycled providing food for worms and aiding soil health as a whole. While man-made fertilisers focus mainly on adding nitrogen, green manures have multiple benefits.

Picking Plants

The way you pick a plant is worth considering for a moment. Harvesting one-crop plants, like carrots, can seem easy. The process becomes more complex when you are harvesting from a plant that you want to keep alive and fruitful for as long as possible.

Picking growth off plants can help them to stay healthy. It allows air flow and prevents disease from taking hold. However, picking has to be balanced with an awareness that the plant needs to be left with enough reserves to keep growing.

For leafy plants such as salad leaves and chard, gently pick leaves from the outer layers of a plant. The heart of the plant will then continue to grow, replacing what has been taken.

Other plants have different requirements but all will need delicate handling so as not to damage future growth. Putting stress on a plant can result in it turning to seed and the premature end of its life.

Be Patient

It is only recently that I have realised I cannot always fix things by quick action. Sometimes other work or lack of time has resulted in not managing to get round to every single job I had planned. This winter I left my beds messy and uncleared. The old plants were battered by frost and weather until the skeletons of summer fell on the earth. They became a natural mulch, offering the soil some defence against the elements. Clover self-seeded and covered many of the beds. I whipped out the occasional stray weeds but that was all.

Our culture leans towards the idea that we should intervene and that our results should be visible. To manipulate and control without really questioning why we are doing what we do. Much of the time I have found you only need to fix things if they have been put out of kilter in the first place.

I first heard about 'no dig' gardening from Charles Dowding, who has been pioneering and trialling this method since the year I was born. On its publication, I immediately bought his book *Organic Gardening: The Natural No-Dig Way* and have since become an absolute fan. In the book he argues that digging – though very occasionally necessary to get rid of weeds or a green manure – damages the soil and is often an unnecessary toil. Instead add compost and let the worms take it down and dig for you. Worms will do a much gentler job.

Sometimes less is more.

6
**Eat Your
Harvest**

I like the word glut. It reminds me of sunshine and takes me to the magical period on a farm when abundance reigns. Vines laden with tomatoes, cratefuls of courgettes and salad by the sackful – the yield of a summer's heat and light is laid at our feet.

Having nurtured, toiled and protected delicate plants through frost, wind, weeds and heat, finally their fragility is temporarily forgotten. Particular crops break into a period of colossal vigour, throwing out their fruits until the harvest exhausts you. This is just a blip in the cycle and a joy of the changing season. It is a time to embrace. The sunshine needs to be stored up to keep us going through sparser months.

Many familiar culinary treats have been born out of this desire and necessity to bottle sunshine that can carry us through the dark months of winter. If we are going to try to eat food that is in season, such preserving techniques enable us to have a taste of those flavours during the cooler months of autumn and winter.

Growing good food seems to attract good cooks and this, for me, is the ideal situation – when the experiences of growing, cooking and eating become completely entwined. In this chapter, some of these wonderful cooks have kindly agreed to share a few of my favourite recipes.

It began with a car ride with my dad. He was telling me how he had just visited Ballymaloe Cookery School in East Cork, Ireland. At about my age, his early twenties, he had spent some time out in California. Now, the people and the spirit at Ballymaloe had taken him right back to that memorable time and he felt it was something I should experience.

On an impulse we decided he should ring up, there and then, to see if I could visit. Darina Allen, who ran the school, was a friend and immediately said yes – the deal being that I would muck in for three weeks and fill spaces if students were absent.

I arrived on Week 9 of a 12-week cookery course. By then, the rest of the students had moved on from soda bread to more refined fare such as sauces and technical pastries. I was completely out of my depth. On arrival Darina gave me a basket of homemade jam and freshly made bread and butter. She sent me off down a rook-filled lane to board with a kind old lady who was the herdsman's mother.

It was the most lovely place to arrive – so perhaps it is unsurprising that it became one of the most difficult to leave.

Ballymaloe was both idyllic and inspiring. With Darina at its helm the cookery school had affected the whole community, providing a platform from which local food and its producers could be celebrated. From this base had emerged a thriving culture of farmers' markets and artisanal production. The most profound and striking thing for me was that many of these producers were young, just a little older than myself.

I worked with Rupert, a grower who gave me a crash course in the art of working farmers' markets in Midleton, Cork and Dublin. We would rise early for picking, driving, setting up and selling. Rupert took the business of selling very seriously. Under supervision, I washed and tore each salad leaf and was made to polish every individual tomato before placing it carefully on display. On the way home I would count the day's takings and we would then head to the Blackbird pub for music and stout.

No one had much money but we ate like kings. We traded paté, fish, chorizo and bread at the markets for our own basil, fresh salad and tomatoes. On sunny days we would sit outside Ballyandreen cottage feasting by the sea, Neil Young's 'Harvest' blaring out the bathroom window.

When autumn came, Rupert and his partner Lydia (who later became his wife) went off to seek winter sunshine. I was left with a bicycle, their poly-tunnel and cottage on the cliff, my friend Pip and Wink the cat.

It was a temporary existence that, through the harsh winter months, became too hard to sustain. Yet the effects of which have never left. I experienced a way of life that strongly resonated with me: a special combination of people, place and work all centred around food and growing.

Recipes

Ballymaloe Sweet Cucumber Pickle

At Ballymaloe I lived in a cottage overlooking the sea that was heated by burning driftwood found on the beach. Despite the basic conditions the fridge was always stocked. Cucumber pickle was a staple currency that complemented other exchanged market fare beautifully.

Serves 8 to 10

—

Ingredients
900g thinly sliced unpeeled cucumber
3 small onions, thinly sliced
350g sugar
2 level teaspoons salt
225ml cider vinegar

Combine the cucumber and onion slices in a large bowl. Mix the sugar, salt and vinegar together and pour over the cucumber and onion. Place in a tightly covered container in refrigerator and leave for at least 4 to 5 hours or overnight before using. Keeps well for up to a week in the refrigerator.

I love this garnished with fresh dill, though it is also delicious garnished with flat leaf parsley or chervil. Capers or pickled nasturtium seeds, see page 122, also complement it very well.

Green Tomato Chutney

For any tomato grower there comes a time where you have to accept defeat. Frost creeps in and leaves you with the last red hues of summer caught in the cold skins of semi-ripe tomatoes. This is not the end but a transition point, when old vines are pulled up and can be replaced by winter salad leaves. Any last fruit (semi-ripe or green) can be picked for savoury feasts later in the year – and used in this delicious recipe.

Makes 12 x 200ml jars

—

Ingredients
1kg cooking apples (*Bramley or Grenadier*), peeled and diced
450g onions, chopped
1kg green tomatoes, chopped (*no need to peel*)
350g white sugar
350g demerera sugar
450g sultanas
2 teaspoons ground ginger
2 teaspoons allspice
2 teaspoons freshly cracked black pepper
2 garlic cloves, coarsely crushed
1 tablespoon salt
900ml white wine vinegar

Put the apples and onions into a wide, stainless-steel saucepan and add the remaining ingredients. Stir well, bring to the boil and simmer gently, uncovered, for about 45 minutes or until reduced by more than half. Stir regularly, particularly towards the end of cooking. Put into sterilised jars and cover immediately with non-reactive lids. Store in a dark, airy place and leave to mellow for at least two weeks before using.

Recipes shared by kind permission of Darina Allen.

Ballycotton Semi-Sun-dried Tomatoes

We used to sell these olive-oil-smothered tomatoes in tubs at the market. It's a good way of using gluts or helping to harness their sweet pungency for a few weeks after the frosts.

Halve the tomatoes (across their middle rather than from their stem looks prettiest). Arrange in one level over a tray, cut side facing upwards. Sprinkle generously with sea salt, sugar and ground black pepper, then drizzle with olive oil. Lay across sprigs of either thyme or rosemary (or both).

Place in a preheated oven, set very low, about 100°C, gas mark 1.

Leave for between four and eight hours depending upon your oven and how 'sun-dried' you like them. The longer you leave them the drier they will become.

These tomatoes are not fully dehydrated so unlike Italian sun-dried tomatoes they should not be kept longer than a couple of days covered in oil and kept in the fridge. They are so useful and delicious that they are easy to use up quickly.

My Best Pesto

A pesto is simply a paste made of basil, but you can use other greens and herbs. Covered by a layer of oil it will keep for some weeks if stored somewhere cool. Pesto is versatile and is delicious with pastas, lamb and other meats.

Home-made pesto is wonderful but will use up a lot of basil. You can replace or supplement the basil with rocket, blanched kale or parsley (though parsley's strength of flavour means you need a lot less leaf in proportion to the other ingredients). My friends at 'Trees Can't Dance' add chilli and wild garlic – all brilliant as a pasta sauce.

Makes 2 x 450g jars

Ingredients
100g fresh basil leaves (*or other greens*)
150ml extra-virgin olive oil
25g fresh pine kernels (*taste when you buy to ensure they are not rancid*)
2 large garlic cloves, peeled and crushed
50g freshly grated Parmesan cheese (*Parmigiano Reggiano is best*)
Salt, to taste

Mix the basil (or other greens) with olive oil, pine kernels and garlic in a food processor or pound in a pestle and mortar.

Remove to a bowl and fold in the Parmesan. Taste and season. Pour into sterilised jars. Cover with a layer of olive oil. Store in the fridge.

Pesto also freezes well but for best results don't add the Parmesan until defrosted.

Pam the Jam

For my brief stint working at River Cottage I was lucky enough to be taken into the warm and foody home of the Corbin family. Pam 'the Jam' Corbin is the queen of all things pickled and preserved. Pickling is one good way of keeping things delicious through the year. Vinegar, sugar and salt all combine to keep things sweet-tasting.

Maddy Corbin has adopted her mum's skills with her 'Pea Green Boat' cooking venture in Edinburgh and has kindly also shared a recipe on page 136 that is good for a glut.

Pam's Runner Bean Pickle

A dead-easy recipe to use up an abundance of beans – long, green runners or short, finer French. It's a lovely recipe which can easily be adjusted to suit your taste; a little less sugar, or a little more, a little chilli to fire it up, a little of cumin's warming tones – just keep in mind the basic ratio of beans, onions, vinegar, cornflour and turmeric.

Makes 5 x 450g jars
—

Ingredients
4 medium-sized onions, peeled and finely sliced
500ml cider vinegar
1kg runner beans
300g demerara sugar
1 heaped tablespoon English mustard powder
1 heaped tablespoon ground turmeric
2 heaped tablespoons cornflour
1–2 tablespoons yellow mustard seed
1 good teaspoon sea salt

Place the onions in a heavy-based pan with 250ml of the vinegar and 250ml of water. Cover and bring to a gentle simmer for approximately 15 to 20 minutes until soft. Remove from heat.

Meanwhile string and prepare the beans by first topping and tailing then finely slicing each bean diagonally into approximately 4–5 cm pieces. Plunge the beans into a large pan of boiling water and return to the boil. Cook the beans for 3 to 5 minutes depending on their age and tenderness – you want your beans to be cooked but to retain a little 'bite'. Remove from heat and strain.

Add the beans to the softened onions with the remaining vinegar then bring to the boil. Add the sugar and stir until completely dissolved.

Place the mustard powder, turmeric, cornflour, mustard seeds and salt in a small mixing bowl and blend to a smooth paste with 100ml of cold water. Stir the spicy paste back into the beans and onions. Keep stirring until the mixture thickens to a glossy smooth sauce. Simmer for a few minutes to allow the cornflour to cook through.

Spoon immediately into warm sterilised jars and seal with vinegar-proof lids.

Pam's Nasturtium 'Capers'

The knobbly green seed pods of the nasturtium flowers have a hot, peppery flavor. They are fun to pickle and can replace the more commonly used seeds from the Capparis plant. The seeds are best collected when they are warm from the sun. Pick only the fresh green or greenish-pink seeds (the yellow older ones will be tough and tasteless).

Use them in home-made tartare sauce, add to tomato salads or to buttery pan-fried fish dishes.

Makes 2 x 113g jars

—

Ingredients
15g sea salt
approx. 100g nasturtium seed pods
A few peppercorns (*optional*)
2 or 3 bay leaves
2 blades of mace
200ml white wine or cider vinegar

Make a light brine by dissolving the salt in 300ml of water. Put the seed pods into a bowl and cover with the cold brine. Leave for 12 to 24 hours (no more). Drain and dry the seed pods.

Place a few peppercorns (if using), a bay leaf and a mace blade into a small sterilised jar. Then pack the seed pods to within 1 cm of the top. Cover the pods with vinegar and seal the jars with vinegar-proof lids. Store in a cool dark place for a few weeks before using. Best used within a year.

Recipes shared by kind permission of Pam Corbin.

'Trees Can't Dance'

My friends Becky and Dan May have a love for all things hot and spicy. Despite living in Northumberland their passion for the tastes of the desert drove them to become some of the world's most northerly chilli growers. Everyone told them categorically that this simply would not work. They refused to be put off and have since proved that, though challenging(!), chillis can be raised far from their native, sunny home. I appreciate this attitude, as they have shown that sometimes it's worth trying things even when everyone tells you otherwise.

They are masters of combining intense flavours in their 'Trees Can't Dance' recipes and have kindly shared a couple of them overleaf.

'Trees Can't Dance' Salsa Verde Piccante

Makes enough for 4 as a side salsa to complement fish, lamb, etc.

—

Ingredients
15g (*handful*) flat leaf parsley leaves, chopped
5g (*small handful*) basil leaves, torn
A few mint leaves, chopped
2–3 tablespoons capers (*or pickled nasturtiums*)
Grated zest of 1 lemon
1 small hot green chilli, deseeded and finely chopped
6 anchovy fillets, drained, rinsed, dried and chopped
1 clove garlic, crushed
1 tablespoon extra-virgin olive oil

—

Optional extras
5g wild garlic leaves, finely chopped, or 5g fresh tarragon

Put all the salsa ingredients into a food processor and pulse briefly for a few seconds. Alternatively mash to a rough paste using a pestle and mortar. Loosen with extra olive oil as required and season with a little salt and pepper.

This salsa is wonderfully robust so don't be afraid to experiment with other herbs – if you have a glut of something, throw it in! My own favourite variations use freshly picked wild garlic leaves or fresh tarragon.

'Trees Can't Dance' Gherkins

Makes a 1kg jar or equivalent jars

—

Ingredients

750g young, small dark-skinned cucumbers, unpeeled but topped
    and tailed
1 fresh bay leaf
½ teaspoon black peppercorns
2 whole garlic cloves
50g sea salt
100ml cider vinegar
4 garlic cloves, peeled and halved
2 sprigs fresh tarragon or dill

Put 600ml of water, the bay leaf, peppercorns, whole garlic
cloves and salt into a small saucepan and bring to the boil.
Remove from the heat and let cool.

Add the vinegar and mix. Place two of the halved garlic cloves
and one of the herb sprigs in the bottom of the sterilised jar.
Pack in the cucumbers, inserting the second sprig of herbs
halfway up the jar. Pour in as much of the pickling liquid
as required to cover the cucumbers, adding the rest of the
garlic towards the top of the jar. The jar should be filled to the
top with cucumbers and pickling liquid. Tightly seal with a
sterilised lid and invert several times to mix.

Let the mixture ferment in a cool, dark place for about one
month. These pickles should be crunchy and with a slightly
sharp taste. Alternatively, speed up the fermentation process
by placing the jar on a sunny window sill for four to five days.
If you take this route the pickles should be refrigerated after
this period.

Fforest Garden Glut Recipes

The beautiful women at Fforest camp in Wales would try to use up all the garden gluts I sporadically bestowed on them – bin liners full of chard, crates and crates of tomatoes, and courgettes that appeared from nowhere overnight.

Anja Fforest Dunk's German Beetroot Salad

Serves 6 to 8

—

Ingredients
1kg beetroot
2 tablespoons vegetable oil
1 tablespoon red wine vinegar
1 teaspoon caraway seeds
1 medium white onion, finely diced
Pinch of salt
Pinch of freshly ground black pepper
Fresh parsley, finely chopped

Cook the beetroot whole in boiling water until tender. Wash in cold water and gentle tease off the outer skin. Slice into 3mm thick rounds.

In a jam jar shake together the oil, vinegar, caraway seeds, onion, salt and pepper.

Pour the dressing over the beetroot while it is still hot and toss. Once the salad has cooled down, sprinkle with the parsley.

This goes well with *klopse* (meatballs).

Sian Tucker's Courgette Fritters

This is a good summer supper when there are plenty of
courgettes in the garden!

Makes about 10 fritters

—

Ingredients
3 medium courgettes, coarsely grated
2 eggs, lightly beaten
6 tablespoons plain white flour
250g block of halloumi, grated
4 spring onions, chopped
1 tablespoon fresh coriander, chopped
½ teaspoon paprika
1 teaspoon ground cumin

Put the coarsely grated courgette in a colander. Sprinkle with
a little salt and leave for 30–40 minutes to drain, then squeeze
well with your hands to release excess liquid.

Meanwhile make a stiff batter with the eggs and flour, crumble
in the grated halloumi and stir in the spring onions, coriander,
paprika and cumin. Season with salt and freshly ground black
pepper and stir well. Finally add the courgettes. The mixture
should be a little moist but not too wet. If you think it's too
wet, simply add a little more flour.

Put a glug of olive oil into a large frying pan and place over
a medium heat. When the oil is hot, scoop up a tablespoon
of the mixture and using a second spoon push it into the
oil. Don't put too many in the pan at once. Four or five fritters
is plenty to cook at a time and you want to avoid them sticking
together. Cook for a couple of minutes. When they seem to be
holding together and browning underneath, turn the fritters
and cook for another 2–3 minutes on the other side.

We like to serve these with either a mint and garlicky yoghurt
raita or a fresh tomato salsa.

Alicia Miller's Fried Tomatoes & 'Gravy'
(also known as 'Pennsylvania Dutch Slumguttle')

My cousin Nathan's wife, Alicia, is from New Mexico. After a day's work in the tunnels at Warborne Farm, Alicia would cook up large, dense Brandywine tomatoes in a 'gravy'. This was perfect comfort food after a hard day's graft. Not a pretty dish, but a great way of making tomatoes the star of a meal and, despite appearances, very delicious. She has kindly shared her recipe below.

Alicia says, 'I like to call this 'Pennsylvania Dutch Slumguttle', because there is no pretty way to plate this dish! My dad's side of the family are Dutch–German immigrants who settled in Pennsylvania. My mum made it regularly after learning it from my grandmother, her mother-in-law.'

For the fried tomatoes

—

Take as many ripe tomatoes as you like, depending on how many you are cooking for.

The recipe is very forgiving so the tomatoes can be firm or tender or even just on the point of going over – but they need to be able to hold their form enough to cut (so not too sloppy).

Blanch them in boiling water for a minute or until the skin breaks, so you can peel and remove the skins easily. Slice them and dredge in flour seasoned well with salt and pepper.

Fry on a medium heat, turning once or twice, in a mixture of butter and oil, until crisp on the outside (more or less) and soft on the inside (the tomato itself should have lost its firmness). You will probably need to do a couple of batches if you are cooking for more than two people. Top up butter and oil as you fry – this is not a low-fat dish.

As you finish cooking the tomatoes, move them into a bowl where they will become a kind of tomatoey mush with some texture – this is fine; they shouldn't hold their shape as they sit.

For the 'gravy'
—

Make a basic white (béchamel) sauce:
2 tablespoons butter
2 tablespoons flour
1 cup of milk
(*double recipe if making for more than 2 people*)

Melt the butter over a medium heat and then add the flour and cook until the mixture is starting to bubble and foam, stirring constantly.

Take off the heat and add milk, whisking with a wire whisk to loosen and incorporate the butter/flour roux into the milk without lumps. Cook gently until the sauce has thickened. If it gets too thick or if you want more sauce, add a further splash of milk and cook a bit more. Season generously with salt and pepper to taste.

Add the tomato mixture and gently incorporate into the gravy, being careful not to break down the tomatoes too much (just poke it with the whisk a little).

For serving, Alicia recommends, 'You must serve this with a side of mashed potatoes for the ultimate in comfort food! The tomato gravy with the mashed potatoes is yum-my!'

Hugh Fearnley-Whittingstall's Pea, Lettuce & Lovage Soup

For a short time I worked in the garden at River Cottage. Hugh F-W, passionate and highly articulate, was on a mission to educate people that the simplest way of sourcing tasty and sustainable food is through using fresh, local, ingredients.

I like this recipe because it challenges the way we think about one of our most common vegetables. While lettuce has become associated with summer salads, it is a cold hardy vegetable that can be grown for much of the year. This soup can suit each season, served piping hot or chilled. I substitute peas with pea shoots (raised in the same way as summer salad plants).

Serves 4

—

Ingredients
1 medium onion, chopped
A little butter or olive oil
250g (*shelled weight*) fresh or frozen peas or pea shoots
1 large cos or 2 large butterhead lettuce
    (*or the outer leaves from four or more lettuces*)
1 litre good chicken or vegetable stock
5 or 6 fresh lovage leaves (*plus a few to garnish*)
    or 3 or 4 sprigs fresh tarragon
Salt and pepper

Sweat the onion in the butter or oil until soft, then add the peas and lettuce leaves.

Pour over two-thirds of the stock, bring to the boil and simmer gently for 4 to 6 minutes.

Remove from the heat and add the lovage leaves or tarragon, then blend the soup with a hand blender or in a liquidiser. How much you blend the soup is a matter of personal preference but it works well both silky-smooth or with a little texture. Again depending on your tastes the soup can be thinned as much as desired with the remaining stock. Season, to taste.

Garnish with lovage, tarragon or pea shoots.

Can be served hot or cold. If reheating, do not allow the soup to boil.

Recipe shared by kind permission of Hugh Fearnley-Whittingstall.

Cardigan Bay Spider Crab Linguine with Rocket Blossom & Parsley

This is a wonderful dish that I had weekly through the crab season when I was living in Wales. In West Wales it was a cheap staple because the main ingredient we had to purchase was the pasta. The spider crab is taking over the waters there. Thus for now they are abundant and sustainable – currently there are plenty more in the sea.

Serves 4 or 5

—

Ingredients

White meat from 2 large spider crabs

500g linguine or other pasta

2 tablespoons olive oil

3 garlic cloves, chopped

½ teaspoon dried chilli flakes

1 tablespoon chopped flat-leaf parsley

Handful of rocket and rocket blossom flowers

Shaving of unwaxed lemon rind (*from half a lemon – or to taste*)

Salt and freshly ground black pepper

Take all the white meat out of the crabs. This is mainly in the enormous legs and claws. I use a rolling pin or a rock to crack the shell. It can be a bit fiddly but the fruits are well worth your labour.

Bring a large pan of water to the boil, salt it well, then add the linguine and cook until al dente. In the meantime warm the olive oil in a pan, add the garlic and sweat until softened. Throw in the chilli. Before the garlic takes any colour add the crab meat and heat through. Season to taste, adding the lemon rind and more chilli if you like, then add the parsley and rocket. Drain the pasta, return it to the pan and add the crab mixture. Toss lightly and serve straightaway.

Hugh Corbin's Mackerel with Summer Veg

A good summer will not only yield a bounty of young sweet veg from the garden, but with luck the salty waters of our shores will bestow a harvest of omega-rich mackerel. This recipe makes a wonderful dish of summery savouriness.

Serves 4

—

Ingredients
75ml olive oil
1 medium onion, sliced
2 or 3 carrots (*150–200g*), sliced
1 fresh sprig thyme, chopped
1 large sprig parsley, finely chopped
200g French beans, trimmed
2 medium tomatoes, peeled, seeded and chopped
2 tablespoons capers or pickled nasturtium seeds (*see page 122*)
4 line-caught mackerel, cleaned – either left whole or filleted
2 tablespoons plain flour
Salt and pepper, to taste

Heat about half of the olive oil in a large, heavy-based, shallow pan. Add the onion, carrot, thyme and parsley and cook over a low heat for about 5 minutes – shake the pan or stir to prevent sticking. Add the beans and cook, stirring frequently, for another 15 minutes. Next add the tomatoes, capers (or nasturtium seeds) and continue to cook for a further 5 minutes until all the lovely flavours have blended.

Lightly dust the mackerel with flour, shaking off any excess. Heat the remaining oil in a frying pan, add the mackerel and cook until golden and the flesh feels soft. Remove with a slotted spoon and place on top of the vegetables. Season to taste.

Serve immediately with a crisp green salad and some crusty bread. Alternatively, this dish is delicious cold, when all the gutsy flavours have mingled quite perfectly together.

'Fields of Plenty' Garden Tomato Sauce

This recipe is a variation from Michael Ableman's Fields of Plenty, *a beautiful book about family farms across North America. Michael helped to establish Fairview Gardens, a 12-acre island of abundant growth surrounded by a sea of concrete in the Santa Barbara suburbs. Fairview is a last bastion of what was once an area of deep top-soils and rich harvest. My visit there made me contemplate the many benefits of growing food near to where people live.*

This sauce can use up your ripest and most imperfect tomatoes. It is a simple recipe that relies upon good ingredients: home-grown tomatoes, olive oil and fresh herbs. Freeze the sauce in meal-size amounts for a winter tomato hit. Can be used for pizza, pasta and many other dishes.

Makes about 950ml

Ingredients

2kg ripe, fragrant tomatoes, peeled, cored and cut into
    1cm thick wedges
6 tablespoons extra-virgin olive oil
1 medium onion, sliced
1 medium carrot, halved lengthwise and cut crosswise into thin slices
Salt, to taste
Chilli pepper flakes, to taste (*optional*)
5 garlic cloves, chopped
1 bunch of fresh basil, chopped (*fresh marjoram or oregano can be
    used instead*)

Blanch the tomatoes in hot water to loosen skins. Peel and chop once cool and discard skins for compost.

Heat a large heavy-bottomed saucepan over a medium heat. Add 3 tablespoons of olive oil, the onion, carrot, and season with a pinch of salt and chilli flakes, if desired. Cover and gently cook for 1 minute, then add the chopped tomatoes and stir to combine. Season with salt (about 1½ teaspoons). Cover again and cook over a medium heat, stirring occasionally, for 30 minutes. Add the basil and cook for 5 more minutes.

Stir in the remaining 3 tablespoons of olive oil, or to taste. If it's too acidic, try adding a pinch of sugar, or, if it's too sweet, a drop of red wine vinegar. If the sauce is too thin, return it to the pot and cook it down until it reaches the desired consistency.

Recipe shared with kind permission of Michael Ableman.

'Pea Green Boat' Sweet Beet Relish

*This delicious relish is a core member of the 'Pea Green Boat'
chutney team. It is sweet and earthy and really captures the
full flavour of the beetroot. It is also very versatile and can be
eaten with salads, sandwiches, cold meats, hot meats, scotch
eggs, cheeses ... the list goes on.*

Makes 8 x 200g jars

—

Ingredients
1kg beetroot
5 large garlic cloves
50ml olive oil
1 tin chopped tomatoes, blended (*though if you have a glut of lovely
tomatoes you could make a tomato purée by sieving roast tomatoes*)
200g red onions, finely chopped or grated
150g radishes, grated
125ml red wine vinegar
60ml balsamic vinegar
250g granulated sugar

Preheat the oven to 180°C/Gas Mark 4. Put the whole washed
beetroots onto a baking tray and cook for 1 to 1½ hours until
they are soft and the skins are beginning to blister. Leave to
cool, and then peel – the skins should come off fairly easily
when rubbed. Coarsely grate the beetroot.

Finely chop or crush the garlic and put in a large pan with the
olive oil. Put over heat and let the garlic flavour infuse the oil
for a few minutes. Stir gently to ensure the garlic does not burn.

Add the tomatoes, onion, radishes, vinegars and sugar.
Stir until the sugar has dissolved. Bring to the boil and simmer
for 10 minutes. Add the grated beetroot and cook for a further
10 minutes until the mixture has thickened. Pour the hot
chutney into warm sterile jars and close the lid immediately.

Use within a year. Refrigerate once opened.

Working on the land has come to be perceived as being far removed from all that is cultural and creative in much of modern society. With industrialisation, diversity is replaced by monoculture, people are replaced by machines, and we are increasingly separated from the land that sustains us. It is an efficient system but one that can have many hidden costs.

Sometimes the work is very hard and you can feel very small in a system where appreciation and pay can be low, but there is another side. The moments of wonder at the beauty around you; having the privilege to witness the detail of nature. I have found my best thoughts happen when working at a steady rhythm in a place where I am immersed in the natural world. There is a pervasive idea that bypassing the need for hard and repetitive work is meant to free humans to become more happy, intellectual and creative beings. Obviously there is a balance, but physical work can create engagement and engagement is central to our experience of life. When my work is physical, I sleep well, have an appetite and my worries fade away.

Agriculture is the foundation stone of human civilisation and I feel it should not be seen as something separate from our cerebral life. We are not separate from nature. Food is a point where humans connect.

A Note on Organic Methods

When my parents first moved to Wales they wanted to come up with a system of farming that looked after the land and cycled resources as much as possible. In doing so, it would be sustainable for the future. This resulted in them and others drawing up some standards to enable this to happen in a way that was visible. The organic movement was attempting to enable the public to have control over how we look after the environment and what we eat. At their bare bones these standards are what we have come to know as the organic standard today.

What we put onto our land affects what we put into our bodies. My parents recognised that soil was at the heart of maintaining the health of the whole. Whatever guises organic has taken, I always come back to this interconnection between soil, body and environment. To understand the world around us, we tend to break it down, but in doing so there is a danger of losing a sense of our wider relationships and how we interconnect.

Soil is a resource that we are fundamentally connected to. It is the source of almost all our food. Keeping soil fertile needs to be done in a way that protects it for the future. Feeding soil through the addition of nitrogen-chemical fertiliser is a wholly unsustainable practice that our conventional farming system relies too heavily upon. It pollutes and uses up world oil capital at a rapid rate.

Organic growing focuses on looking after your soil as a whole rather than applying quick fixes for things that may be deficient or cause disease. Soil needs to be nurtured otherwise it can be damaged or even lost through compaction, pollution, erosion or salination. In the UK we stand to lose five tonnes of top-soil per hectare per year because of the way we farm. This is wasting soil reserves, a legacy that took thousands of years to build. We are using up a gift that does not solely belong to us.

Carbon Sink

The other secret held by our seemingly humble soil is that it is a massive carbon sink, holding more carbon even than our oceans. Cultivating soil allows the oxidation of carbon, which contributes to climate change. Organic systems try to minimise the release of carbon and instead focus on returning carbon to the soil (in the form of organic matter: compost and plants). In doing this we can slow down climate change while also improving the structure and fertility of this vital resource. This all may sound a little complex and you may be thinking, 'How does this relate to me and my patch?' Really it is about being conscious of our place in the larger system and we can do this from anywhere. If we harvest food from our gardens we can abide by the law of return. Composting organic waste converts it into something that is useful.

Specialisation and Separation

In a world where we have become increasingly detached from our food source, buying organically certified food is a way of gaining control over the systems we support. It is a legal term – unlike 'fresh', 'local', etc. – so it is regulated. However, the need for the legislation of 'organic' food is also in part a symptom of us having accepted detachment from the food we eat.

We can all reconnect and challenge this separation

by forging more direct connections, with local farms and farmers and through the way we choose to shop. Or by growing things ourselves.

The beauty of a farmers' market, box schemes and community-supported agriculture is you can talk directly to the producers, ask questions and even visit the farms. I share the view of Mr Woody Guthrie: 'This is your land, and this is my land.' We are all responsible and more powerful than we think. We steward the land in the choices we make every time we eat.

It comes down to knowledge. There are many questions in an un-transparent world: Who produces food? How are these workers treated? It may be grown organically but where has it come from and what was involved: unfair pay, vast quantities of water, aeroplanes, refrigerators, centralised storage depots? And what happens if no one buys it – will it end up in landfill?

Shopping at farmers' markets or buying locally through box schemes helps to break down the barriers separating us from how and where food is produced. Growing our own takes this one step further.

The 10 Commandments of a Grower

1. Diversity builds health

2. Diversity builds resilience

3. Remember the law of return
   – compost and cycle fertility

4. Think for the future
   – invest in the soil and sow for the next season

5. Observe nature and you will learn as you 'Do'

6. Use what you have
   – make waste useful and use the resources on your doorstep

7. Adapt to your context
   – both its advantages and disadvantages

8. Water is life
   – try to harness and preserve this precious resource

9. Nurture your soil and it will nurture you

10. Food is the way to people's hearts

Side Shoots

COMPANION PLANTS

Some plants can benefit from being grown alongside others.
Here are some useful combinations.

For good use of space:
Tomatoes with basil (under cover)
Cucumbers with dill
Courgettes with climbing French or runner beans – courgettes
also give ground cover which minimises weed growth.

For pest control and attracting pollinators:
Tomatoes with tagetes (Chinese marigolds) – as their scent
deters whitefly.
Nasturtiums – position at the corners of your vegetable patch to
draw blackfly and other pests away from your crops.

For green manures:
White clover or trefoil with tomatoes, peppers, aubergines,
cucumbers, courgettes, kale and purple sprouting broccoli – not
only do these low-growing green manures prevent weed growth,
they also fix nitrogen and act as a moisture-maintaining mulch.
    When your veg crop has been harvested, dig the white clover
or trefoil into the soil to add nitrogen and organic matter which
will benefit any follow-on crops – or leave in as ground cover
over winter. They will begin fixing nitrogen again in spring when
temperatures rise.

GARDENING CALENDAR

When to sow and grow

The following advice is not gospel. Where you live and the weather conditions will make each place and year unique. Some things I have labelled 1st, 2nd, 3rd, etc., because their shorter yielding lifespan means these crops can be planted a few times (in succession) through the season to allow continual harvest. Other crops just require one sowing. If labelled 'under cover' start off in module trays indoors or in a greenhouse.

February

Early: Sow 1st lettuce, 1st rocket, under cover.
Mid: Sow tomatoes inside (need heat*, see over). Try to get them in around Valentine's Day.
Late: Sow 1st spinach under cover; sow broad beans (from now sow every 3 weeks until mid March).

March

Early: Sow 1st true spinach, 1st beetroot, 1st chard, 1st perpetual spinach, 1st parsley, 1st coriander, 1st chervil, 1st dill, all under cover. Sow basil (needs heat*).
Mid: Sow 2nd lettuce and 2nd broad beans, thyme and marjoram; sow 1st French beans.
Late: Take cuttings of rosemary, sage.

April

Early: Sow 2nd true spinach, under cover.
Mid: Sow cucumbers indoors; sow courgettes (need protection from frost).

May

Early: Sow 2nd beetroot.
Mid: Sow 2nd French beans.

June

Early to mid: Sow 2nd chard, 2nd perpetual spinach, 2nd parsley, 2nd chervil, 2nd dill and 2nd coriander.

July

Early: Sow 3rd beetroot, 3rd lettuce, 1st endives and 1st chicories, purple sprouting broccoli and kale.
Mid: Sow 3rd French beans.

August

Early: Sow 3rd chard, 3rd perpetual and 3rd true spinach.
Early to mid: Sow all 1st winter salad, 3rd dill, 3rd parsley, 3rd chervil and 3rd coriander.
Late: Sow 4th French beans.
All August sowings are best planted out under cover or in a greenhouse.

September

Early: Sow 4th lettuce.

After this point falling temperatures mean that it is generally not worth sowing any more crops until the following February. Broad beans are an exception as they can be sown in November (see note on page 86).

Any bare ground that does not have crops in can be sown with a green manure over winter (see page 104). Most green manures should be sown by early September so they can establish themselves before it gets too cold. If you miss this window, rye is useful as it can be sown as late as early to mid October.

Plants marked with an asterisk (*) need a relatively constant heat to germinate – temperatures of around 20°C dropping to 16°C at the lowest. They can survive some temperature fluctuation but should not go below 16°C at night so need to be indoors or set on a propagation heat mat. The rest do not need heat, though will benefit from warmth and generally do need protection from frost.

First sowing dates are a rough guide. Light levels from the hours of daylight should be sufficient to support the growth of specific seeds from this point onwards.

The other main variable condition affecting plants is heat. If you start plants in a greenhouse you give them some protection from cold. However, frost can still affect young seedlings. If you can start plants off in a house this is not a problem – however, here they will have less light. It is a bit of a balancing act between these two essential plant requirements. Sowing seeds early means a potentially earlier harvest. However, if a spring is particularly cold or has late frosts this can prove to be a gamble unless you can offer the necessary protection from the cold through planting them out into a greenhouse, covering with fleece/bubble wrap, or not planting out in the ground until temperatures rise.

Though this unpredictability can be frustrating, it puts us immediately in touch with the elements and our surrounding environment. If it was all controlled like a lab (which some greenhouses now are!) for me it would take away some of the excitement, instinct, connection and variation. In terms of a calendar there is not a single right date to plant because every context and year is different.

RESOURCES

Useful Books

For information:
*Forgotten Skills of
Cooking*, Darina Allen
(Kyle Cathie, 2009)

*Preserves: The River Cottage
Handbook No. 2*, Pam Corbin
(Bloomsbury, 2008)

*Charles Dowding's Vegetable
Course*, Charles Dowding
(Frances Lincoln, 2012)

Tender: Volume 1, Nigel Slater
(Fourth Estate, 2009)

For inspiration:
Fields of Plenty, Michael Ableman
(Chronicle Books, 2005)

Silent Spring, Rachel Carson
(Penguin Classics, 2000.
First published 1962)

The One Straw Revolution,
Masanobu Fukuoka
(NYRB Classics, 2009.
First published 1978)

Small is Beautiful, E. F. Schumacher
(Vintage, 2011. First published 1973)

The Fat of the Land, John Seymour
(Carningli Books, 2008.
First published 1975)

Film Documentaries

The Real Dirt on Farmer John
Director: Taggart Siegel
2005

Food, Inc.
Director: Robert Kenner
2008

Useful Websites

For information:
gardenorganic.org.uk
soilassociation.org
landshare.net
sustainweb.org
sustainablefoodtrust.org
sustaination.co
localharvest.org (USA)
growingcommunities.org

For seed:
realseeds.co.uk
tamarorganics.co.uk
gardenorganic.org.uk

For inspiration:
cookingisfun.ie
dolectures.com
departmentofsmallworks.co.uk
wwoof.org
coldatnight.co.uk

About Me

I began a career of farming and growing serendipitously in the scorching summer of 2003. Footloose and unsure of my path after university, I didn't know what I wanted to do. As a stopgap I returned to Bwlchwernen, the farm where I had grown up. Extra hands were needed with the carrot weeding, as well as the summer harvest at Blaencamel, a neighbouring farm. I invited four close friends to join me – all at a similar crossroads. What I hadn't realised at the time was that this was the exact journey my parents had made 30 years earlier.

During those summer months the combined elements of being with friends, working on the land and the heat of the season created a time of great contentment – a happy existence of hard work, good food and company in a place that I loved. Standing by the poly-tunnel after a dusty afternoon's work, I considered for the first time that perhaps this experience could be more than a bridge between education and the 'real' world of work.

Going back might have felt regressive at first, but the years spent away allowed me to see things afresh. What did I want my career to mean to me? At last I knew that I wanted to do something that could really benefit land and people. Here at home I stumbled upon it, right where I began.

So this was the beginning of my journey as a farmer and a grower. It has taken me against the traffic of recent generations who have left the land in their droves and has led to some interesting places – the romantic and the downright grim. From the woods of Vancouver Island, to two years in a yurt in a Cotswold village. At times it has been very hard – both the physical nature of the work and society's judgement that you must be some kind of simple being. But ten farms later I'm still standing and I continue to love my work. I hope this book will show you that you don't have to be an expert to share in the joy of growing, picking and cooking something of your own.

On the eve of leaving rural Wales to move back to London, I was keen to bring what I have learned with me. I have been fortunate and now work for Growing Communities, an award-winning social enterprise based in Hackney, who run an organic box scheme, farmers' market and urban food production sites. I am now head grower at their four acre starter farm in Dagenham, east London.

Supper has come to be dictated by what I have growing outside. There is no reason to leave this logic behind just because I have less space. I know that continuing to grow food will give me the sustenance I need, as nurturing even the smallest vegetable patch is a way of nurturing myself.

I have been battling with the decision between urban and rural life. This is my way of challenging the great divide. I hope you may share in the harvest.

Alice Holden

Bwlchwernen Fawr, Summer 2003

Thanks

Thank you first and foremost to David and Clare Hieatt for offering me their apples that day and providing me with a wonderful Welsh home.

This book would never have happened without Miranda West's faith and hard work. Thanks for setting me deadlines and sorry that I did not always make them. Thanks also to Nick Hand for the lovely photographs and many lifts. And to designer Wilf Whitty and illustrator Millie Marotta.

I am grateful to the the farmers / growers: Will Johnson, Pete Richardson, Anthony Hinks, Steven Carroll, Lyn Phillips, Pete Fox, Rupert Hugh-Jones, Nathan Richards, Anne Evans, Peter Seggar, Mike Brook, Iain Tolhurst, Michael Abelman and Charles Dowding – for their passion and openness to sharing knowledge.

Thanks also to the cooks: Dan and Becky May, Darina Allen, Hugh F.-W., Michael Ableman, Sian Tucker, Anja Fforest Dunk, Alicia Miller and Maddy, Pam and Hugh Corbin who allowed me to share recipes in this book.

Thanks also to Patricia Ross, Amani Omejer, Garfield Lindsay Miller, the Fforest team, the Corbin family and the inhabitants of Coleshill – especially Tom for becoming a 'farmitect'.

Thanks to Nick Rebbeck and my friends for making the farm so much fun that beautiful summer.

And finally, Mum and Dad, I am grateful that you challenged convention and headed west to Bwlchwernen 40 years ago.

Index

INDEX